ANNUAL 2019

US
POLITICS

Anthony J. Bennett

HODDER
EDUCATION
AN HACHETTE UK COMPANY

Hodder Education, an Hachette UK company, Blenheim Court, George Street, Banbury, Oxfordshire OX16 5BH

Orders
Bookpoint Ltd, 130 Park Drive, Milton Park, Abingdon, Oxfordshire OX14 4SE
tel: 01235 827827
fax: 01235 400401
e-mail: education@bookpoint.co.uk

Lines are open 9.00 a.m.–5.00 p.m., Monday to Saturday, with a 24-hour message answering service. You can also order through the Hodder Education website: www.hoddereducation.co.uk

ISBN 978-1-5104-4758-5

First printed 2019

Impression number 5 4 3 2 1

Year 2022 2021 2020 2019

Typeset by Integra Software Services Pvt. Ltd., Pondicherry, India

Cover photo: Christos Georghiou/Adobe Stock

Printed by CPI Group (UK) Ltd, Croydon, CR0 4YY

Hachette UK's policy is to use papers that are natural, renewable and recyclable products and made from wood grown in well-managed forests and other controlled sources. The logging and manufacturing processes are expected to conform to the environmental regulations of the country of origin.

Contents

Contents

Chapter 1

The 2018 midterm congressional elections

What you need to know

- Midterm elections come halfway through a president's four-year term of office.
- Therefore, they fall in years 2010, 2014, 2018 and so on.
- In these years, there are elections for all 435 members of the House of Representatives, one-third of the Senate, as well as numerous state governors and legislators.
- The president's party usually loses seats in midterm elections.

Before the elections

As 2018 dawned, the Republican Party still controlled both houses of Congress — just. The House of Representatives was comfortably within their control with a 47-seat majority, there being 241 Republicans and 194 Democrats. But in the Senate, with the loss of the special election in Alabama at the end of 2017, the Republican majority had dwindled from four (52–48) to just two (51–49). All this meant that the Democrats would need to make overall gains of 24 and 2 seats respectively in the House and the Senate to regain the majorities.

Retirements

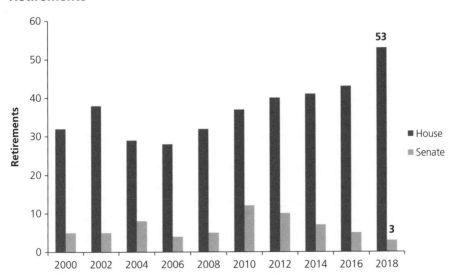

Figure 1.1 Retirements in the House and Senate, 2000–18

In the Senate, the 33 seats last contested in 2010 were up for re-election, plus two special elections – in Minnesota and Mississippi – to complete the final two years of the terms of two senators who had resigned earlier in the year. Thus there were 35 Senate races scheduled for the 2018 midterms. Of those 35 seats, 24 were held by Democrats, 2 by independents who caucus with the Democrats, and just 9 by Republicans. That made the Democrats' chances of winning the overall 2 seats they needed for the majority unusually difficult. They would have to hold all their 26 seats and win two of the other nine races. On the retirement front, the Republicans were again at a disadvantage. Just three incumbent senators announced they would not seek re-election in 2018 – Jeff Flake of Arizona, Bob Corker of Tennessee and Orrin Hatch of Utah – all Republicans (see Figure 1.1).

Congressional primaries

The 2018 congressional primaries saw the fewest primary defeats since 2008 – just four, all in the House of Representatives (see Figure 1.2). For the third successive cycle, no senators lost in the primaries. The four House members to lose primaries were two from each party – Democrats Mike Capuano of Massachusetts and Joe Crowley of New York, and Republicans Robert Pittenger of North Carolina and Mark Sanford of South Carolina.

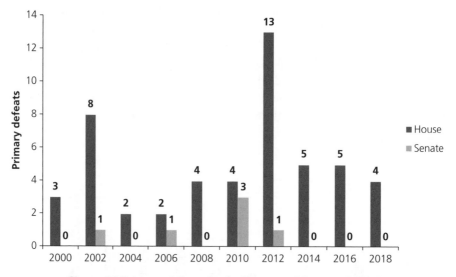

Figure 1.2 Primary defeats in the House and Senate, 2000–18

The two most interesting primary defeats were those involving Mark Sanford and Joe Crowley, as they both tell us something about the state of their respective parties. Sanford served two terms as governor of South Carolina (2003–11). In 2009, he disappeared for six days – eventually returning from Argentina to admit an adulterous relationship. Four years later, Sanford was elected to the House of Representatives where he had served for six years before his time as governor. Although Sanford supported Trump during the 2016 election, he soon became one of the President's most vocal Republican critics. Just before the 2018 primary,

Trump tweeted that Sanford was 'nothing but trouble' and 'very unhelpful'. Sanford lost to state representative Katie Arrington by 46% to 51% after Arrington had been endorsed by Trump. But Arrington went on to lose the district to the Democrats in November. Trump's support does not always mean winning.

Joe Crowley was a ten-term Democrat representing parts of the Bronx and Queens in New York City — an area just to the north of JFK airport. In the last Congress, he served as chair of the House Democratic Caucus, making him the fourth-ranking member of the House Democratic leadership team. Delivering this stunning defeat was 28-year-old Alexandria Ocasio-Cortez who, according to the *New York Times*, won on the basis of 'demographic and generational change, insider versus outsider, traditional tactics versus modern-age digital organising'. Crowley's district had changed in the redistricting following the 2010 census and become much more racially diverse and younger. You could get a flavour of their differences by watching the YouTube videos they both posted in the days running up to the primary. Crowley boasted that 'I can put myself in other people's shoes', while Ocasio-Cortez said she was the 'girl from the Bronx'. He was pictured driving round the district in a car; she rode the subway. On Twitter, his video had 90,000 views by Primary Day; hers had 500,000! Ms Ocasio-Cortez went on to win this safe Democrat seat with 78% of the vote.

Senate races

We have already seen that of the 35 Senate races in the 2018 election, 24 were being defended by Democrats and just 9 by Republicans. The remaining 2 were held by independents who usually vote with the Democrats. That immediately gave the Republicans a distinct advantage. Furthermore, 8 of the 9 Republican-held seats were in states that Donald Trump had won in 2016. Only Dean Heller of Nevada was running in a 2016 Clinton state.

Table 1.1 Democrat senators running in 2018 in states won by Trump in 2016

Democratic senator	State	Trump winning margin 2016 (percentage points)	Senate result 2018
Bill Nelson	Florida	1	Republican gain
Joe Donnelly	Indiana	19	Republican gain
Debbie Stabenow	Michigan	1	Democrat hold
Claire McCaskill	Missouri	19	Republican gain
Jon Tester	Montana	20	Democrat hold
Heidi Heitkamp	North Dakota	36	Republican gain
Sherrod Brown	Ohio	9	Democrat hold
Bob Casey	Pennsylvania	1	Democrat hold
Joe Manchin	West Virginia	43	Democrat hold
Tammy Baldwin	Wisconsin	1	Democrat hold

But things were even harder for the Democrats, as 10 of their incumbents were running in states that Donald Trump had won two years earlier (see Table 1.1). For four senators, Trump had won their state by just 1 percentage point, but five Democrats were defending their seats in states where Trump had won in a landslide. In West Virginia, for example, Trump had beaten Clinton by 69% to 26%. All of the four Democrats who lost on Election Night were defending their seats in Trump states – Bill Nelson, Joe Donnelly, Claire McCaskill and Heidi Heitkamp. It was impressive that three of the four lost only by single-digit percentages.

Table 1.2 Results of Senate elections, 2018

State	Winner	Party	%	Opponent	Party	%
Arizona	Rep. Kyrsten Sinema	D	49	*Rep. Martha McSally	R	48
California	**Dianne Feinstein**	D	54	Kevin de León	R	46
Connecticut	**Chris Murphy**	D	59	Matthew Corey	R	40
Delaware	**Tom Carper**	D	60	Robert Arlett	R	38
Florida	Gov. Rick Scott	R	50	**Bill Nelson**	D	49
Hawaii	**Mazie Hirono**	D	71	Ron Curtis	R	29
Indiana	Mike Braun	R	52	**Joe Donnelly**	D	44
Maine	**Angus King**	Ind	54	Eric Brakey	R	35
				Zak Ringelstein	D	10
Maryland	**Ben Cardin**	D	64	Tony Campbell	R	31
Massachusetts	**Elizabeth Warren**	D	60	Geoff Diehl	R	36
Michigan	**Debbie Stabenow**	D	52	John James	R	46
Minnesota	**Amy Klobuchar**	D	60	Jim Newberger	R	36
Minnesota (S)	**Tina Smith**	D	53	Karin Housley	R	42
Mississippi	**Roger Wicker**	R	59	David Baria	D	39
Mississippi (S)	**Cindy Hyde-Smith**	R	54	Ex-Rep. Mike Espy	D	46
Missouri	Josh Hawley	R	51	**Claire McCaskill**	D	45
Montana	**Jon Tester**	D	50	Matt Rosendale	R	47
Nebraska	**Deb Fischer**	R	58	Jane Raybould	D	38
Nevada	Rep. Jacky Rosen	D	50	**Dean Heller**	**R**	45
New Jersey	**Bob Menendez**	D	53	Bob Hugin	R	44
New Mexico	**Martin Heinrich**	D	54	Mick Rich	R	31
				Gary Johnson	Lib.	15

State	Winner	Party	%	Opponent	Party	%
New York	**Kirsten Gillibrand**	D	66	Chele Farley	R	33
North Dakota	Rep. Kevin Cramer	R	55	**Heidi Heitkamp**	D	45
Ohio	**Sherrod Brown**	D	53	Rep. Jim Renacci	R	47
Pennsylvania	**Bob Casey**	D	56	Rep. Lou Barletta	R	43
Rhode Island	**Sheldon Whitehouse**	D	61	Robert Flanders	R	38
Tennessee	*Rep. Marsha Blackburn	R	55	Ex-Gov. Phil Bredesen	D	44
Texas	**Ted Cruz**	R	51	Rep. Beto O'Rourke	D	48
Utah	*Ex-Gov. Mitt Romney	R	62	Jenny Wilson	D	32
Vermont	**Bernie Sanders**	Ind/D	67	Lawrence Zupan	R	27
Virginia	**Tim Kaine**	D	57	Corey Stewart	R	41
Washington	**Maria Cantwell**	D	59	Susan Hutchison	R	41
West Virginia	**Joe Manchin**	D	50	Patrick Morrisey	R	46
Wisconsin	**Tammy Baldwin**	D	55	Leah Vukmir	R	45
Wyoming	**John Barrasso**	R	67	Gary Trauner	D	30

Bold = incumbent
* = incumbent party in open seat
(S) = special election

The only incumbent Republican casualty of Election Night was Dean Heller, who lost by 5 percentage points to Democrat House member Jacky Rosen. But in the open race in Arizona to replace Republican Jeff Flake, Representative Kyrsten Sinema came with a late run in the absentee ballot count to defeat her House colleague Martha McSally by just under 40,000 votes out of over 2 million cast. So with 4 gains and 2 losses, the Republicans came out of these elections with an overall gain of just 2 seats, meaning that the party balance in the new Senate in January 2019 will be 53 Republicans and effectively 47 Democrats. And although President Trump made some quite audacious claims about what a stunning victory this was, he might have done well to recall that President George W. Bush's Republicans also won two Senate seats in the 2002 midterms (see Table 1.7). So it's not that unusual.

Table 1.3 Senators: retired, defeated, re-elected, 2000–18

Year	Retired	Sought re-election	Defeated in primary	Defeated in general election	Total re-elected	% re-elected who sought re-election
2000	5	29	0	5	24	82.8
2002	5	28	1	3	24	85.7
2004	8	26	0	1	25	96.1
2006	4	29	1	6	23	79.3
2008	5	30	0	5	25	83.3
2010	12	25	3	2	21	84.0
2012	10	23	1	1	21	91.3
2014	8	28	0	5	23	82.1
2016	5	29	0	2	27	93.1
2018	3	32	0	5	27	84.4

In terms of representation, the new Senate will have 23 women members — 16 Democrats and 7 Republicans — the highest it has ever had. It marks some progress in that 40 years ago there were no women in the Senate at all, and even 20 years ago there were just 9.

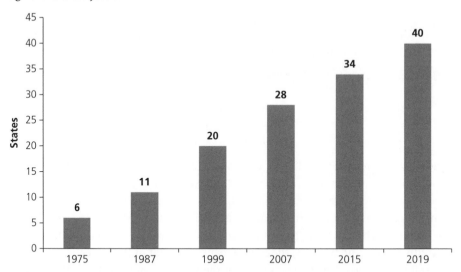

Figure 1.3 Number of states in which both senators are from the same party, 1975–2019

Figure 1.3 shows how partisanship has increased over recent decades. Nearly five decades ago, in only 6 states did both senators come from the same party. By 2007, that figure had risen to 28. But in January 2019, 40 states will have two senators from the same party. Indeed, it is this fact that made the re-election of Democrats Jon Tester (Montana), Sherrod Brown (Ohio), Bob Casey (Pennsylvania), Joe Manchin (West Virginia) and Tammy Baldwin (Wisconsin) quite surprising.

For not only are the other senators from their states all Republicans, but Donald Trump won the presidential race in their states in 2016.

House races

The Democrats came into these elections needing to win at least 24 seats to regain the majority in the House of Representatives that they lost following the 2010 midterm elections. It soon became clear on Election Night that they would, as expected, achieve that. And by the time the dust had settled the Democrats ended up with 234 seats in the new House to 201 for the Republicans. They gained 43 seats from the Republicans (see Table 1.4) and lost 3 (see Table 1.5), giving them an overall gain of 40 seats. That made 2018 the Democrats' best result in House midterm elections since 1974 – the elections held just three months after the resignation of President Nixon over Watergate (see Table 1.7).

Table 1.4 House seats gained by Democrats from Republicans

House district	Incumbent/race status	2016 presidential winner
Arizona 2	Open	Clinton +4.9
California 10	Jeff Denham	Clinton +3.0
California 25	Steve Knight	Clinton +6.7
California 39	Open	Clinton +8.6
California 45	Mimi Walters	Clinton +5.4
California 48	Dana Rohrabacher	Clinton +1.5
California 49	Open	Clinton +7.5
Colorado 6	Mike Coffman	Clinton +8.9
Florida 26	Carlos Curbelo	Clinton +16.3
Florida 27	Open	Clinton +19.6
Georgia 6	Karen Handl	Trump +1.5
Illinois 6	Peter Roskam	Clinton +7.0
Illinois 14	Randy Hultgren	Trump +3.9
Iowa 1	Rod Blum	Trump +3.5
Iowa 3	David Young	Trump +3.5
Kansas 3	Kevin Yoder	Clinton +1.2
Maine 2	Bruce Poliquin	Trump +10.3
Michigan 8	Mike Bishop	Trump +6.7
Michigan 11	Open	Trump +4.4
Minnesota 2	Jason Lewis	Trump +1.2
Minnesota 3	Erik Paulsen	Clinton +9.4
New Jersey 2	Open	Trump +4.6
New Jersey 3	Tom MacArthur	Trump +6.2
New Jersey 7	Leonard Lance	Clinton +1.1
New Jersey 11	Open	Trump +0.9
New Mexico 2	Open	Trump +10.2

House district	Incumbent/race status	2016 presidential winner
New York 11	Dan Donovan	Trump +9.8
New York 19	John Faso	Trump +6.8
New York 22	Claudia Tenney	Trump +15.5
Oklahoma 5	Steve Russell	Trump +13.4
Pennsylvania 5	Open	–*
Pennsylvania 6	Open	–*
Pennsylvania 7	Open	–*
Pennsylvania 17	Keith Rothfus	–*
South Carolina 1	Mark Sanford (defeated in primary)	Trump +13.1
Texas 7	John Culberson	Clinton +1.4
Texas 32	Pete Sessions	Clinton +1.9
Utah 4	Mia Love	Trump +6.7
Virginia 2	Scott Taylor	Trump +3.4
Virginia 7	Dave Brat	Trump +6.5
Virginia 10	Barbara Comstock	Clinton +10.0
Washington 8	Open	Clinton +3.0

* Pennsylvania's House district boundaries were ruled unconstitutional in January 2018 and redrawn. This makes comparisons with 2016 impossible.

Table 1.5 House seats gained by Republicans from Democrats

House District	Incumbent/race status	2016 presidential winner
Minnesota 1	Open	Trump +14.9
Minnesota 8	Open	Trump +15.6
Pennsylvania 14	Open	–*

* See note to Table 1.4.

As Table 1.4 shows, 19 of these 43 gains came in districts won by Hillary Clinton in the 2016 presidential race. Another 9 came in districts where Donald Trump won by less than 5 percentage points in 2016. But five Democratic House gains came in districts won by President Trump by 10 percentage points or more just two years earlier — Maine 2, New Mexico 2, New York 22, Oklahoma 5 and South Carolina 1. In 2016, Steve Russell had won Oklahoma's 5th District by over 20 percentage points, while Trump carried the district by 13 points. Yet Democrat Kendra Horn defeated Russell by 1 percentage point this time around. It was the first time the Democrats had won the district since 1974. The three districts that switched from the Democrats to the Republicans were districts won by Trump in 2016 (see Table 1.5).

As a result, there are now just 32 'split districts' left across the country — 30 that voted for Trump in 2016 but have a Democrat representative in the House, and just 2 that voted for Clinton in 2016 but still have a Republican representative. Just ten years ago, in 2008, there were 83 such split districts. Back in 1984, there were 196! This just shows the hyper-partisanship of American politics today. Today's American voters tend to vote either straight Republican or straight Democrat when it comes to the White House and the House of Representatives. Split-ticket voting is somewhat a thing of the past.

Table 1.6 House members: retired, defeated, re-elected, 2000–18

Year	Retired	Sought re-election	Defeated in primary	Defeated in general election	Total re-elected	% re-elected who sought re-election
2000	32	403	3	6	394	97.8
2002	38	397	8	8	381	96.0
2004	29	404	2	7	395	97.8
2006	28	405	2	22	381	94.1
2008	32	402	4	19	379	94.3
2010	37	396	4	54	338	85.4
2012	40	390	13	27	350	89.7
2014	41	394	5	13	376	95.4
2016	42	393	5	8	380	96.6
2018	54	381	4	30	347	91.0

There were some huge swings to the Democrats in some suburban districts in the Northeast. In New Jersey's 11th District, for example, the Republicans, who had won the seat 58–39 in 2016, lost it 43–56 in 2018. Likewise, in New York's 11th District, Republican incumbent Dan Donovan lost to his Democratic opponent by 6 percentage points despite winning 62–36 just two years earlier. As a result, New York City now has no Republican House members for the first time since 1932.

At the time of writing it looked likely that 103 women had been elected to the House in 2018 – easily beating the previous record of 84 in 2015–16. Of the 35 new women House members, all but one is a Democrat. Of the 103 women House members in the new Congress, 88 are Democrats and 15 Republicans. This means that both chambers will have 23% women members.

Table 1.7 Gains/losses by president's party in midterm congressional elections, 1982–2018

Year	Party holding presidency	Gains/losses for president's party in:	
		House	Senate
1974	R	−48	−4
1978	D	−15	−2
1982	R	−26	+1
1986	R	−5	−8

Year	Party holding presidency	Gains/losses for president's party in:	
		House	Senate
1990	R	−8	−1
1994	D	−52	−8
1998	D	+5	0
2002	R	+5	+2
2006	R	−30	−6
2010	D	−63	−6
2014	D	−13	−9
2018	R	−40	+2

Who won and why?

'Tremendous success tonight. Thank you to all!' tweeted President Trump late on Election Night. Some might think 'success' a curious description for the worst midterm House results for his party in over four decades. Presumably the President was focusing more on the gains in the Senate. But whereas after most elections it is fairly easy to attribute success and failure, the 2018 midterms don't really fit into that pattern. I am sure that in a moment of unvarnished honesty, the President would admit that he would have liked to have avoided many of those losses in the House. And given the very favourable political map – and a very favourable economy – he might have wished for more gains in the Senate. States such as Montana and West Virginia should surely have dropped into his party's column if the night had been a true success.

For the Democrats, the much-vaunted 'blue wave' did not really materialise. Although the House results were encouraging, there were still some Republicans who survived whom the Democrats had surely hoped to defeat. And no election which involved them losing ground in the Senate – against such a controversial incumbent president – could really be described as a victory. So let's try to draw together some explanations and lessons by asking the question 'Why didn't the Democrats perform better?' We can suggest five important reasons.

Because of how the electorate was made up

Democrats had placed their hopes on the fact that President Trump was especially unpopular among two groups of voters – women and young voters. They were to be the key to the blue wave – to mix metaphors. And, as Table 1.8 shows, the Democrats certainly did well with these two demographic groups. Democrats won 59% of women's vote and 67% among 18–29-year-old voters. Both figures were up on 2016. Indeed, the Democrats benefited from a 12 percentage point increase in their support among young voters compared with 2016. So why did these increased levels of support fail to deliver the victories for which Democrats were hoping?

Table 1.8 Who voted for whom: 2016 and 2018 compared

Category (% of the electorate)	2018		2016		Increase for Dems since 2016
	Rep. (%)	Dem. (%)	Trump (%)	Clinton (%)	
Men (48)	51	47	53	41	+6
Women (52)	40	59	42	54	+5
Whites (72)	54	44	58	37	+7
African-Americans (11)	9	90	8	88	+2
Hispanics/Latinos (11)	29	69	29	65	+4
Asian (3)	23	77	29	65	+12
White men (35)	60	39	63	31	+8
White women (37)	49	49	53	43	+6
Black men (6)	12	88	13	80	+8
Black women (6)	7	92	4	94	−2
Hispanic/Latino men (5)	34	63	33	62	+1
Hispanic/Latino women (6)	26	73	26	68	+5
Married (59)	47	51	53	43	+8
Non-married (41)	37	61	38	55	+6
Married men (30)	51	48	58	37	+11
Married women (29)	44	54	47	49	+5
Non-married men (18)	44	54	45	46	+8
Non-married women (23)	31	66	33	62	+4
Aged 18–29 (13)	32	67	37	55	+12
Aged 30–44 (22)	39	58	42	50	+8
Aged 45–64 (39)	50	49	53	44	+5
Aged 65+ (26)	50	48	53	45	+3
White 18–29 (8)	43	56	48	43	+13
White 30–44 (15)	48	48	55	37	+11
White 45–64 (29)	59	40	63	34	+6
White 65+ (22)	56	43	58	39	+4
High school graduate (23)	51	48	51	45	+3
Some college education (25)	47	52	52	43	+9
College graduate (25)	45	54	45	49	+5
Post-graduate (17)	34	65	37	58	+7
White non-college (41)	61	37	67	28	+9
White non-college men	66	32	72	23	+9
White non-college women	56	42	62	34	+8
White college grad (31)	45	53	49	45	+8
White college grad men	51	47	54	39	+8
White college grad women	39	59	45	51	+8

Category (% of the electorate)	2018		2016		Increase for Dems since 2016
	Rep. (%)	Dem. (%)	Trump (%)	Clinton (%)	
Population of area:					
City over 50,000 (32)	32	**65**	35	**59**	+6
Suburbs (51)	49	49	**50**	45	+4
Small town/rural (17)	**56**	42	**62**	34	+8
Democrats (37)	4	**95**	9	**89**	+6
Republicans (33)	**94**	6	**90**	7	−1
Independents (30)	42	**54**	**48**	42	+12
Liberal (27)	8	**91**	10	**84**	+7
Moderate (37)	36	**62**	41	**52**	+10
Conservatives (36)	**83**	16	**81**	15	+1
Family income:					
Under $30,000 (17)	34	**63**	41	**53**	+10
$30,000–49,999 (21)	41	**57**	42	**51**	+6
$50,000–99,999 (29)	47	**52**	**50**	46	+6
$100,000–199,999 (25)	**51**	47	**48**	47	0
$200,000 and over (9)	**52**	47	**48**	47	0

Bold = winner

Source: Pew Research Centre

The answer comes when one looks at the make-up of the electorate. In 2016, women made up 52% of voters. And for all their vociferous opposition to Trump, for all the women's protest marches, for all the #MeToo campaigns, for all the women candidates, in 2018 women still made up 52% of those who voted.

Young voters gave Democrats one of the highest levels of support of any demographic group. They gave them a 35 percentage point lead over the Republicans in voting support. The 67% support they gave to the Democrats was even higher than in the first Obama election of 2008. But in that election, 18–29-year-olds constituted 18% of those who voted. In 2018 they made up just 13%. Put simply, young voters just don't turn up for the midterms in anything like the proportions that they do for presidential elections. And that's been a trend running for decades. So why didn't the Democrats perform better? Because they didn't manage to increase the proportions of women and young people turning out to vote, especially in the battleground states.

Because the economic landscape was against them

We have already seen that in the Senate races, the political landscape was clearly against the Democrats. But the economic landscape posed a much bigger hurdle to success for Democratic candidates in both Senate and House races. When exit polls asked voters about the condition of the national economy, 68% thought it was excellent or good while only 31% said it was not so good or poor. And, as Table 1.9 shows, these figures are almost the exact opposite of what they were two years ago. It's very difficult for a challenging party to win elections in good economic times.

Table 1.9 Exit poll data on the economy

Q: How would you describe the condition of the national economy?			
Rating	% agreeing 2018 (2016)	Dem. (%)	Rep. (%)
Excellent	17 (3)	12	87
Good	51 (33)	47	51
Not so good	23 (41)	83	15
Poor	7 (21)	85	8
Excellent/Good	68 (36)	39	60
Not so good/Poor	31 (62)	83	14

Source: cnn.com/election/2018/exit-polls

Furthermore, 36% of voters told pollsters that they thought their family's financial situation was better compared with two years ago. And of that 36%, 77% voted for Republican candidates. Only 14% of voters thought their finances had got worse during the Trump years — and Democrats won 80% of the votes among that much smaller group. Here was another reason Democrats didn't do as well as they had hoped.

Because Trump had no coattails in the House in 2016

First, let's define our terminology. The term 'coattails effect' is used to describe the effect when an extremely popular candidate at the top of the election ticket carries candidates for lower offices with him/her into office. So if Trump had coattails in 2016, we would have seen significant Republican gains in the House in 2016. But that's not what we saw at all. In fact, as Table 1.10 shows, Trump was the first president since JFK in 1960 to win office and yet see his own party lose seats in the House.

What often happens is that a newly elected president sees large gains in the House for his party. This happened in 1980, 1992 and 2008. But then in the next midterms — 1982, 1994 and 2010 — the opposition was able to win many of those seats back again. Hence the Democrats picked up 26 House seats in 1982, whilst the Republicans gained 54 House seats in 1994 and 63 in 2010. So the Democrats faced a much more difficult task in 2018 because there were no 'easy pickings' for them from the President's coattails in the previous election cycle. Indeed, in the circumstances, the Democrats' overall gain of 40 House seats in these midterms was a staggering success.

Table 1.10 Gains/losses in House elections by incoming presidents, 1960–2016

Year	President	Party	House seats won/lost by his party	House seats won/lost at the next midterms by his party
1960	John Kennedy	D	−21	−4
1968	Richard Nixon	R	+5	−12
1976	Jimmy Carter	D	+1	−15
1980	Ronald Reagan	R	+26	−26
1988	George H.W. Bush	R	+7	−8
1992	Bill Clinton	D	+54	−52
2000	George W. Bush	R	+8	+5
2008	Barack Obama	D	+21	−63
2016	Donald Trump	R	−6	−40

Because Trump was successful in motivating his political base

It's often the case that in the first midterm election of a presidency, the president's party makes up a smaller proportion of the electorate than it did two years earlier. For example, in 2008, Obama's Democrats constituted 39% of the electorate. But two years later, that fell to 36%. But this did not occur for Trump's Republicans in 2018. Back in 2016, Republican identifiers accounted for 33% of voters in the exit polls. In 2018, it was still 33%. What is more, Trump actually increased his share of the Republican vote – from 90% in 2016 to 94% in 2018, which is, I believe, the highest level of support for any president or presidential candidate since President Reagan's 97% among Republicans in 1984.

How did Trump get his political base motivated during the campaign? The answer – Kavanaugh and caravans. At the beginning of the campaign, the President used the controversy surrounding the nomination of Judge Brett Kavanaugh to the Supreme Court as red meat for the Trump base. After all, when pollsters asked voters in 2016 whether nominations to the Supreme Court were a factor in deciding their vote, 21% said it was the most important factor, and 56% of those voted for Trump. It was something of an irony that the controversy over Kavanaugh – stoked by Democrats on Capitol Hill – probably worked to the advantage of the President and his party.

And then there was the 'caravan' of Central American migrants heading for Mexico and then, apparently, for the US border. Trump talked of an 'onslaught' on America's borders by 'criminals'. In the final rallies of his campaign in such states as Texas and Indiana, Trump accused the Democrats of wanting to 'invite caravan after caravan' of asylum seekers to the United States, adding that 'a blue wave will equal a crime wave, and a red wave will equal law and safety'.

Yes, it certainly rallied the Trump base, but not without its own costs. For such rhetoric made the job of Republican candidates in America's more wealthy suburbs much more difficult. It probably cost Republican congressman Chris Coffman his seat in the suburbs of Denver, Colorado. 'Republicans don't like us,' said Alaa Shaker, a 26-year-old Iraqi immigrant. 'They like people who look like them.' Coffman's Democratic opponent said he wanted to see the House hold hearings on what he called 'the dangerous policies and very dangerous rhetoric' of the President and his administration. Coffman lost the race by 11 percentage points. Two years earlier, he had won the race by 8 points.

Because the voting trends helpful to Democrats were not apparent in the battleground states

This should sound familiar. After all, it was really the story behind the 2016 presidential election in which one candidate won the popular vote but, because those votes were not cast in sufficient numbers in the key battleground states, the other candidate won in the Electoral College. There's always a danger in analysing American elections that we think of them as one big national election. But they're not. They are a collection of 50 separate state elections. Let me give you two clear examples of what we mean here.

First, regarding gender: Table 1.8 tells us that women supported Democratic candidates by 59% to 40% — a huge 19 percentage point advantage. The trouble is that this advantage was far more apparent in some states than in others. In California, for example, Democrats enjoyed a 30-point advantage amongst women voters. But the Senate race in California was a shoo-in for the Democrats anyway. In the battleground state of Indiana, that advantage amongst women shrunk to just 3 points — 49 to 46 — which is one reason why the Democrat senator Joe Donnelly lost.

Second, regarding age: nationwide, 18–29-year-olds voted for Democrats over Republicans 67%–32%. But in Indiana, the same demographic group actually gave Republicans 49% support to 44% for the Democrats. The moral to the story was that big margins nationally were not always reflected in battleground states. And Democrats will need to find ways to overcome these problems if they are not to suffer a similar fate in 2020.

What can we learn from the 2018 midterm elections?

There were, of course, elections being held other than those for Congress. The Democrats made an overall gain of seven in the governors' races and won over 300 state legislative seats. But these did no more than begin to repair the damage from the Obama years when Democrats suffered huge losses in state governments. So what lessons can we draw overall? Here are three takeaways.

Both parties are weak

At a time of prosperity at home and (relative) peace abroad, the Republicans should not have been losing 40 seats in the House, especially having failed to gain any two years earlier. But with such a profoundly divisive and unpopular president, the Democrats should have given the Republicans a good 'shellacking' — in the House, the Senate and the state races. But neither party seems able to break out of its own self-imposed 'base'. True, the Democrats' base may be a bit bigger than the Republicans' base, but even they failed to deliver a convincing victory. Exit polls showed that voters disliked the Democrats less than they disliked the Republicans (see Table 1.11), but neither party enjoys the approval of even a majority of voters. The Democrats were better at setting the agenda of these elections. Their principal theme of healthcare was what the voters said was important to them — not immigration, the favourite topic at President Trump's pre-election rallies (see Table 1.12). After the 2016 election, we wrote of a 'coalition of resentment' being largely responsible for Trump's victory. All one can say is that this resentment remains largely unaddressed. Neither party really knows what its true identity is. Neither party seems able to reach out and build a new winning coalition .

Table 1.11 Voters' views of the two major parties

Q: What is your opinion of —		
The Democratic Party	Favourable	48%
	Unfavourable	47%
The Republican Party	Favourable	44%
	Unfavourable	52%

Table 1.12 Exit poll data on the most important issue facing the country

Q: What is the most important issue facing the country?			
Issue	% agreeing	Dem. (%)	Rep. (%)
Healthcare	41	75	23
Immigration	23	23	75
The economy	22	34	63
Gun policy	10	70	29

The Democrats still don't know how to address Trump and Trumpism

When it comes to 2020, the Democrats still don't know how to take on Trump and win. Ought they to move further to the radical left, or ought they to move more to the traditional middle ground which seems to lie vacant? Ought they to nominate a Bernie Sanders or a Joe Biden? The Democrats still really don't know. Ought they to go male or female? Cory Booker or Elizabeth Warren? Ought they to go with someone of colour or a white American? Kamala Harris or Kirsten Gillibrand? And they're going to have to fight a bitter presidential primary battle in early 2020 to decide which it will be. Who best to take on President Trump? Often, as we emerge from the midterm elections, one or two clear front-runners become obvious in the challenging party. But not this year.

The economy may be key for the next two years

There's a danger that the media will focus on the Trump distractions – of which there will doubtless continue to be many. But it's highly unlikely that any of these things will move a significant number of voters from their current position regarding the President – either in support or in opposition. Exit polls found that 46% of voters already 'strongly disapproved' of Donald Trump. More voters thought his trade policies hurt their local economy (29%) than helped it (25%). Nearly half of voters (46%) thought the President's immigration policies were 'too tough'. More voters said that his foreign policy made them feel 'less safe' (46%) than 'safer' (38%). More opposed his appointment of Brett Kavanaugh to the Supreme Court than supported it.

But the one thing that could significantly affect Donald Trump's support in the next two years is if the economy were to turn sour. Rather like in the late 1990s with Bill Clinton, voters are prepared to overlook a lot of things they don't like about a president provided they feel that – to quote Ronald Reagan – they are 'better off than they were four years ago'. So who will be asking the Ronald Reagan question in 2020? Who will look the camera in the eye and ask, 'Are you better off than you were four years ago?' If President Trump and his Republicans can do that, he still stands a chance of a second term. If it's the Democrats asking that – because they know the answer for most would be 'no' – then the President would in all probability be toast.

Questions

1 What happened in terms of retirements from Congress in 2018?
2 How many members of Congress were defeated in primaries in 2018?
3 Write a brief summary of the 2018 Senate elections.
4 What do the data in Figure 1.3 tell us about partisanship in US politics today?
5 What do the data in Tables 1.4 and 1.5 tell us about the 2018 House races?
6 What are 'split districts'? How many were there (a) in 2008; (b) after the 2018 midterms?
7 Analyse the data in Table 1.7.
8 What important facts do the data in Table 1.8 tell us about voting trends in 2018?
9 Give four reasons why the Democrats didn't perform better in the 2018 midterms.

Chapter 2

Where does power reside in Congress?

What you need to know

- Congress is made up of two houses: the House of Representatives and the Senate.
- In both houses there are important committees where much of the legislative and scrutiny functions are carried out.
- Both houses also have two party leadership teams — one for each major party — which include majority and minority leaders, plus — in the House — the Speaker, who is a partisan leadership figure.
- Different parties can control each chamber and it is also possible for the president's party to control neither of the two houses of Congress.

Introduction

These days, Congress is often derided as a weak, dysfunctional and somewhat powerless body. One has only to pick out some titles of recently published books on Congress: *The Broken Branch* (2008), *Unorthodox Congress* (2011), *Why the U.S. Congress is so Dysfunctional* (2013), *Broken: Can the Senate Save Itself and the Country?* (2018). But are things really as bad as all that? Has it merely become fashionable to deride Congress as ineffective when sometimes its inactivity is a result of exactly what the Constitution's framers wanted — limited government based on the doctrine of 'separated institutions sharing powers' (Richard Neustadt)?

In this chapter we shall look at four possible answers to the question 'Where does power reside in Congress?' — in the Senate, in the House of Representatives, in the committee rooms, in the party leadership. And we shall draw things together with a short case study of one of Congress's landmark pieces of legislation during the current Congress — the Tax Cuts and Jobs Act of 2017.

The Senate

Of course, all the textbooks will tell you that the Senate is more powerful than the House. But that is dealing with the assigned powers of the two bodies and the fact that the Senate has a number of significant exclusive powers. And 'powers' and 'power' are two different concepts. 'Powers' are those tasks assigned to a particular office or body, while 'power' is about the ability of that body or those who hold that office to get things done. To put it another way: 'powers' are about theory; 'power' is about practice. But powers can — and often do — lead to power. So it is not surprising that power resides in the Senate, especially when we are talking about something like the confirmation of executive and judicial appointments.

Since the inauguration of President Trump in January 2017, the Senate has been less willing than one might have presumed — for a Republican-controlled chamber — to nod through Trump's executive branch nominees. By June 2018, of the 20 individuals nominated to lead one of the 15 executive departments, two have withdrawn from the process after the Senate made it fairly clear that their confirmation was unlikely. The two individuals were Andrew Puzder, who was nominated to be secretary of labor in December 2016 but withdrew in mid-February 2017, and Ronnie Jackson, who was nominated to be secretary of veterans affairs in March 2018 but withdrew a month later. That was two cabinet-level nominations withdrawn in the first 15 months of Trump's administration. To put that in perspective, President George W. Bush suffered only two withdrawals in his entire eight years in office.

Of the 18 heads of executive departments that were nominated by President Trump during this period, 11 had more than one-third of the Senate voting against their confirmation. Three — Attorney General Jeff Sessions, Health and Human Services Secretary Tom Price and Secretary of the Treasury Steve Mnuchin — attracted 47 'no' votes in the final Senate vote. Secretary of Education Betsy DeVos even required the casting vote of the Vice President to get her nomination confirmed — 51–50.

Meanwhile, among sub-cabinet-level nominations, there were 17 withdrawals following significant reservations being raised by senators, plus withdrawals of those nominated as United States ambassadors to Belgium, Singapore and South Korea.

In mid-June 2017, the President nominated former Republican House member Scott Garrett to be president of the Export–Import Bank of the United States. While serving in Congress, Garrett had not only been a vocal critic of the bank but had suggested that it ought to be abolished. Senator Sherrod Brown, a Democrat from Ohio and the ranking minority member of the Senate Banking Committee which would hold hearings on Garrett's nomination, voiced his surprise at Trump's choice, suggesting that no Democrat would support him. But when the Senate Banking Committee came to vote on the nomination six months later, not only did all the Democrats vote 'no', so did Republicans Mike Rounds of South Dakota and Tim Scott of South Carolina, thereby sinking the nomination by 13 votes to 10. Clearly when it comes to executive branch nominations, the power resides in the Senate.

The Senate likewise bared its teeth when it came to Trump's nominations to the federal judiciary. After a severe mauling by the Senate Judiciary Committee, three of President Trump's nominees to the federal judiciary withdrew. The most high profile of these was Matthew Petersen, formerly the chairman of the Federal Election Commission and nominated by the President to be a trial judge in the United States District Court for the District of Columbia. The Q and A exchange between Petersen and Republican senator John Neely Kennedy of Louisiana went viral on YouTube (see Box 2.1). Three days after that exchange, Petersen withdrew. Here again, the Senate was seen as powerful.

Box 2.1 Exchange between Senator John Neely Kennedy and Matthew Petersen, Senate Judiciary Committee, 13 December 2017

Kennedy: Mr Petersen, have you ever tried a jury trial?

Petersen: I have not.

K: Civil?

P: No.

K: Criminal?

P: No.

K: Bench?

P: No.

K: State or federal court?

P: I have not.

K: Have you ever taken a deposition?

P: I was involved in taking depositions when I was an associate at Wiley Rein [a law firm] when I first came out of law school. But that was —

K: How many depositions?

P: I'd be struggling to remember.

K: Less than ten?

P: Yes.

K: Less than five?

P: Probably somewhere in that range.

K: Have you ever taken a deposition by yourself?

P: I believe not. No.

K: Okay. Have you ever argued a motion in state court?

P: I have not.

K: Have you ever argued a motion in federal court?

P: No.

K: Do you know what the Younger abstention doctrine is?

P: I've heard of it, but I —

K: How about the Pullman abstention doctrine?

P: I — I —

K: You'll see that a lot in federal court.

But what when it comes to legislation? Here again, the Senate may well have significant power where the numbers game is important. With only 100 members, you need just 51 votes to make a majority. When the Senate is pretty evenly divided between the two major parties — as it has been during

Trump's first two years – individual members find they have quite a bit of leverage to gain concessions when it comes to amending major pieces of legislation. For most of Trump's first year, the Republicans enjoyed a 52–48 seat majority in the Senate. But after they lost the special election in Alabama in December 2017, this was reduced to a 51–49 split. That meant that the Republican leadership in the Senate could afford no more than one of its members voting against its legislation if no Democrats were supporting it. That gave considerable clout to individual Republican senators. So, for example, Senator Marco Rubio of Florida was able to wring significant concessions from his party leadership on the child tax credit when it came to the passage of the President's flagship tax cuts bill at the end of the year.

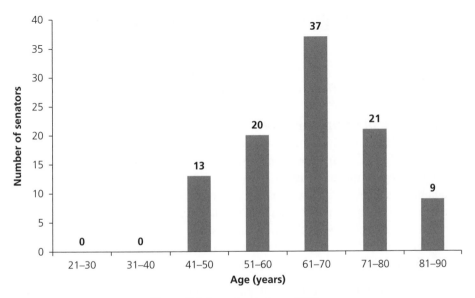

Figure 2.1 Age of senators, 2018

A quick digression before we leave the Senate. Given the high rates of re-election that senators have enjoyed in recent decades and the fact that around half of the members came to the Senate after a fairly lengthy stint in the House, the Senate has become a somewhat senile body. Well over half the members are over 60 years old, and almost one-third are over 70. Nine are over 80! (See Figure 2.1.) Put another way, nearly half of the senators were born during the presidencies of Franklin D. Roosevelt (1933–45) and Harry S. Truman (1945–53) whilst just one was born during the administration of Jimmy Carter (1977–81). (See Figure 2.2.) Senator Tom Cotton of Arkansas was born less than four months into Carter's single term of office. At the other end of the scale, Dianne Feinstein of California was born just three months into Roosevelt's first term in 1933.

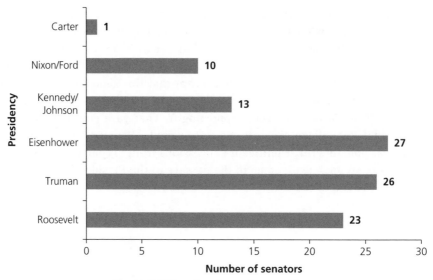

Figure 2.2 Senators born: by presidency

The House of Representatives

Because of the rules in the House, the majority party is heavily favoured. So in Trump's first two years, Democrats had little influence in the House in terms of either legislation or scrutiny. This was exacerbated by the numbers – the Republicans enjoying a 47-seat majority. The House, however, has suffered of late from a partisan and fractured Republican majority. Its partisan nature meant that it sometimes passed legislation which a less partisan Senate did not then follow through. So, for example, in May 2017 the House voted to repeal and replace Obamacare – but this legislation then died in the Senate.

The fractured nature of the House Republicans has been a cause of much difficulty to both the last two Republican speakers – John Boehner and Paul Ryan. Both saw their party caucus snatch defeat from the jaws of victory on a number of pieces of legislation simply because their fractured caucus could not muster the votes to defeat the Democratic minority. Even on something as high profile and important as President Trump's tax cuts, 12 moderate Republicans voted 'no'. At other times it has been the conservative wing of the party that has jeopardised action, most notably the 30 or so members of the Freedom Caucus.

The House majority will often try to enhance its power by limiting the influence that minority party members have over legislation by the use of what are known as 'closed rules'. Most bills coming out of committee and moving to the floor of the House for their full debate need to pass through the House Rules Committee. This committee sets the priority of bills by awarding a rule which sets out the rules for debate – stating, for example, whether any amendments can be made to the bill at this stage. A bill needs a rule to progress to the floor of the House. Box 2.2 sets out the main types of rule that the Rules Committee can award. Clearly the minority party in the House will favour an open rule while the majority party will favour structured or closed rules, allowing it to dictate the content and shape of the bill by its party majority.

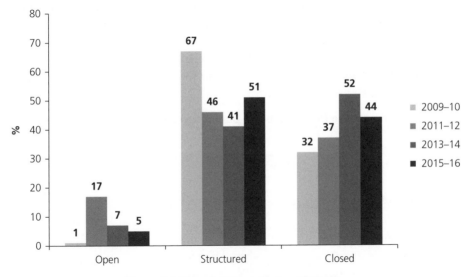

Figure 2.3 Use of different rules, 2010–16

But as Figure 2.3 shows, over the eight years between 2009 and 2016 the vast majority of rules awarded by the Rules Committee were structured or closed rules – in excess of 90% in three of these four congressional sessions. And we can add two further points. First, both parties used the same strategy, for when the Democrats controlled the House in 2009–10 the pattern was very similar to when the Republicans have controlled it in the years since. However, Democrats would want to point out that 2009–10 marked the low point (32%) for the awarding of closed rules. Second, the preliminary figures for 2017–18 indicate that the Republicans have continued to use a high proportion of closed rules.

The committee rooms

It seems fairly clear even to the neutral observer that the power of the committees – especially the standing and select committees – has been jeopardised by the partisan way in which the Republicans have conducted business. This has been especially true in terms of some committees and in terms of their scrutiny function. It has also been more noticeable since President Trump's arrival in the White House.

Nowhere has this been seen more clearly than in the House Permanent Select Committee on Intelligence. Here, a group of Republican House members led by the committee chairman Devin Nunes of California led a concerted campaign to prove a case of corruption at both the Department of Justice and the FBI, and to undermine the investigation of Special Counsel Robert Mueller, egged on by the Trump White House. The effect of this was to neutralise any political clout that the committee might have had as the Democratic members of the committee – led by the Democrats' senior member, Adam Schiff – refused to go along with much of the committee's activities.

The effectiveness of the standing committees in the House has also been undermined by the Republican Party's term-limit of three terms on committee chairmanships. Of the 19 standing committee chairs in post in 2018, eight have already announced that they will not seek re-election in the 2018 midterm elections (see Table 2.1) and five of those would have had to relinquish their chairmanships had they been re-elected and the Republicans maintained their majority in the House.

Table 2.1 Republican House Standing Committee chairs not seeking re-election in 2018

Committee	Chairman	State
Appropriations	Rodney Frelinghuysen	New Jersey
Financial Services	Jeb Hensarling	Texas
Foreign Affairs	Ed Royce	California
House Administration	Gregg Harper	Mississippi
Judiciary	Bob Goodlatte	Virginia
Oversight and Government Reform	Trey Gowdy	South Carolina
Science, Space and Technology	Lamar Smith	Texas
Transportation and Infrastructure	Bill Shuster	Pennsylvania

As we saw earlier, one could make a strong case for suggesting that the Senate standing committees are a significant repository of congressional power, especially in their oversight function. But this may change in 2019 with Democrats taking control of the House.

Party leadership

The term 'party leadership' in Congress can be drawn either widely or narrowly. In its widest sense, it would include not only the House Speaker, the Senate's president pro tempore, and the majority and minority leaders of both houses, but also the party whips, the party committee chairs and the standing committee chairs of both chambers. Here, however, we will use the term in its narrowest sense – to refer to the Senate majority and minority leaders, the House Speaker and the House minority leader. In terms of personalities during 2018 that has meant Senators Mitch McConnell and Chuck Schumer, Speaker Paul Ryan and Congresswoman Nancy Pelosi.

This is hardly a leadership team with a new car smell. Their average age – even including the 48-year-old Ryan – is over 67. McConnell is 76 and Pelosi 78. If re-elected in the midterms, Pelosi will be 80 during the next Congress. Together they have amassed 123 years of service on Capitol Hill between the four of them. Chuck Schumer was first elected to Congress with Ronald Reagan in November 1980. McConnell joined him four years later, and Pelosi in 1987. Certainly on television, McConnell and Pelosi look somewhat languid and past their 'best before' dates.

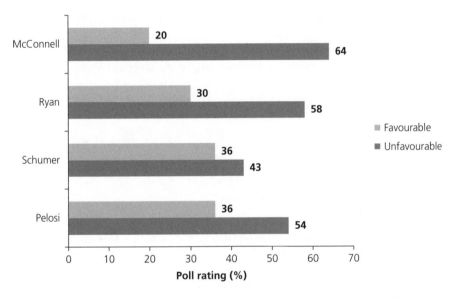

Figure 2.4 Favourability ratings of congressional leadership, 2018

Nor are any of them held in high esteem by the electorate. As Figure 2.4 shows, all had higher unfavourable than favourable ratings in opinion polls – ranging from a deficit of just 7 points for Schumer and 18 points for Pelosi, to 28 points for Ryan and a massive 44 points for McConnell. Put simply, that clearly makes the Democratic leadership less disliked than the Republican leadership. But regardless of the public disapproval of the party leadership in Congress, the short case study with which we close this chapter may show that this is actually where the power in Congress resides today.

Case study: the Tax and Jobs Act (2017)

The Tax and Jobs Act (2017) – in congressional jargon 'HR1' – was more commonly known as the Trump tax cut. According to the President, the ensuing tax cuts were 'huge' – Trump's favourite adjective. The comparative hugeness of the tax cuts was much debated but one thing was indisputable: as far as the bill itself was concerned, it was huge! The final version that passed the Senate in December was 479 pages long. That's huge.

There used to be an apocryphal story in Washington that involved a senator being reported to his party leadership for killing a snail that had invaded his suite of offices on Capitol Hill. 'Why did you do such a cruel and horrid thing?' the senator was asked. Came the reply: 'It annoyed me so. It just followed me around all day!' Given the usually snail-like pace of action in Congress and the size of this bill, you might presume that it took months — maybe over a year — to pass. You may, therefore, be surprised to hear that the bill passed through the entire legislative process in both houses and was signed into law by the President in just 50 days (see Table 2.2).

Table 2.2 Passage of Trump's tax cuts through Congress, 2017

Date	Action
2 November	Bill introduced in House; referred to Ways and Means Committee
6–7 November	Committee holds hearings on bill
13 November	Reported out of committee
15 November	Granted rule by House Rules Committee for four hours' debate
16 November	Passed by House: 227–205 (R: 227–13; D: 0–192)
27 November	Bill introduced in Senate
30 November	Senate begins consideration on floor
1 December	Ten roll call votes on Democratic (minority) amendments to commit bill to Senate Finance Committee — all lost on party-line votes
2 December	Bill (with Republican amendments) passed by Senate: 51–49 (R: 51–1; D: 0–48)
4 December	House rejects Senate amendments; requests a conference committee
13 December	Conference committee meets
15 December	Conference committee issues report
19 December	House debates and votes on conference report; agrees to new version of bill: 227–203 (R: 227–12; D: 0–191)
20 December	Senate debates and votes on conference report; makes further amendment and passes 51–48 (R: 51–0; D: 0–48)
20 December	House agrees to Senate amendment: 224–201 (R: 224–12; D: 0–189)
21 December	Bill sent to President
22 December	Bill signed into law by President Trump

The House passed the bill after just two days of committee hearings followed by debate on two days. In the Senate, the bill never reached the relevant committee, but was dealt with in a single week — starting on the Monday and passed by the Saturday. After the House rejected the Senate amendments, it took nine days to set up a conference committee, but once that was done, Congress wrapped up the whole thing in a week. But how was this possible? The answer is because the whole process was being driven by the Republican White House, House Speaker Ryan and Senate majority leader McConnell. All five 'passage' votes — three in the House and two in the Senate — were strict party-line votes. Not a single Democrat voted for the bill in either house. Twelve House Republicans voted against the bill on three occasions; one cast just one 'no' vote but voted 'yes' on the other two occasions. Eleven of those 12 came from California, New York or New Jersey, eight belonged to the Republican Main Stream Partnership — a moderate/centrist caucus — and three were Republicans from districts that Hillary Clinton had won in 2016.

The other major clue to the level of control exercised by the congressional party leadership was the membership of the conference committee that was appointed to resolve the differences between the House and Senate versions of the bill. Of the 17 Republican members of the conference committee, nine were members of the party leadership either as committee chairs or as elected members of the leadership team in their chamber. It was the same for the Democrats. Of their 12 conferees, eight were members of the party leadership either as ranking minority members of a committee or as elected members of their party leadership. This means that just shy of 60% of conferees were part of the congressional party leadership teams. That's where the power resides in Congress.

Questions

1 How has the Republican-controlled Senate attempted to check President Trump in terms of appointments?
2 What does the author mean by 'the fractured nature of the House Republicans'?
3 What is the significance of the data shown in Figure 2.3?
4 How has the effectiveness of congressional standing committees been undermined?
5 Explain the significance of the data shown in Figure 2.4.
6 What conclusions do you draw about where power resides in Congress from the case study on the Tax and Jobs Act (2017)?

Chapter 3

What's the Supreme Court been deciding in 2017–18?

What you need to know

- The Supreme Court is the highest court in the USA.
- The Court is made up of nine justices, appointed by the president, for life.
- The Supreme Court has the power of judicial review. This is the power to declare Acts of Congress or actions of the executive branch — or acts or actions of state governments — unconstitutional, and thereby null and void.
- By this power of judicial review, the Court acts as the umpire of the Constitution and plays a leading role in safeguarding Americans' rights and liberties.

The 2017–18 term of the United States Supreme Court was the first for three years which ran its full course with a full complement of nine justices on the bench. After Justice Antonin Scalia died on 13 February 2016 the Court had only eight members until Neil Gorsuch joined the Court on 8 April 2017. But that had meant that both the 2015–16 and the 2016–17 terms ran much or most of their time with only eight justices. That said, as the switch of Gorsuch for Scalia was probably like for like in terms of the justices' judicial philosophy, we were not expecting any significant shift in the Court's ideological balance in 2017–18 from what it had been back in 2014–15 when the Court last had its full complement of justices.

Because the Court was back to full strength, the 2017–18 term featured more potentially landmark cases. In this chapter we shall consider five of them — three concerning First Amendment rights, one considering Fourth Amendment rights, and the fifth relating to presidential power (see Table 3.1).

Table 3.1 Selected Supreme Court decisions, 2017–18 term

Case	Concerning	Decision
Masterpiece Cakeshop v *Colorado Civil Rights Commission*	Freedom of speech/religion (First Amendment)	7–2
National Institute of Family and Life Advocates v *Becera*	Freedom of speech/religion (First Amendment)	5–4
Janus v *American Federation of State, County and Municipal Employees*	Freedom of speech (First Amendment)	5–4
Carpenter v *United States*	Freedom from unreasonable searches (Fourth Amendment)	5–4
Trump v *Hawaii*	Presidential power	5–4

First Amendment: gay rights meet religious freedom

In what was undoubtedly the Court's marquee decision of this term, the justices had to adjudicate the rights of two different groups of people and how the freedoms of one group might infringe the freedoms of the other. It was a classic debate about societal freedom – the rights of the LGBT community versus those of orthodox Christians. And it all revolved around a wedding cake.

Briefly, the background to the case. In 2012, Charlie Craig and David Mullins, two residents of Colorado, decided to marry, but because same-sex marriages were not at that time legal in their state, they decided to travel to Massachusetts for the ceremony but return to Denver for the reception. In July 2012, Craig and Mullins arrived at the Masterpiece Cakeshop in Lakewood, just to the west of Denver. There they spoke with Jack Phillips, the cake shop proprietor who, as soon as he learnt that the cake was to celebrate a same-sex marriage, told the couple that he didn't make cakes to celebrate such occasions because of his Christian beliefs. Phillips recalled that the whole conversation lasted just about 20 seconds. 'Sorry guys, I don't make cakes for same-sex weddings', he told them. He added that they were welcome to buy any baked goods which were for sale in his store. But Craig and Mullins quickly left with no further conversation and no purchase. Another bakery provided the cake for Craig and Mullins, but the couple decided to file a complaint with the Colorado Civil Rights Commission under the state's anti-discriminatory law. Both the state trial and appeal courts found in favour of Craig and Mullins, but when the Colorado Supreme Court declined to hear a further appeal on behalf of Mr Phillips, he took the case to the US Supreme Court, where it arrived as *Masterpiece Cakeshop* v *Colorado Civil Rights Commission*.

In its decision, the Supreme Court ruled (7–2) that owner Jack Phillips' First Amendment rights had been infringed, though the ruling was extremely narrow and will doubtless lead to similar challenges which hopefully will bring about a greater degree of clarity. The Court's ruling focused almost exclusively on the religious bias shown by the Colorado Civil Rights Commission members rather than on the First Amendment rights of Phillips per se. Doubtless the narrowness of the decision was the ingredient that brought seven votes to the majority side, made up of the conservative quartet of Roberts, Thomas, Alito and Gorsuch, plus the votes of two of the Court's liberals – Stephen Breyer and Elena Kagan – plus swing justice Anthony Kennedy, who authored the opinion.

What we learnt, therefore, in this decision was more about the mistakes which the members of the Colorado Civil Rights Commission made, rather than anything definitive about how the rights of the gay community can be compatible with those who hold orthodox religious beliefs. Much was made of the Commission's statement that religious beliefs have been 'used to justify all kinds of discrimination throughout history, whether it be slavery, whether it be the holocaust'. Such statements, said Justice Kennedy in the majority opinion, 'cast doubt on the fairness and impartiality of the adjudication of Phillips' case'. Kennedy added: 'The Civil Rights Commission's treatment [of Phillips] has some elements of a clear and impermissible hostility toward the sincere religious beliefs that motivated his objection.' The trouble is, this begs the question: 'If the civil rights commissioners in Colorado had not used prejudicial language, would the same decision have been allowed to stand?'

But although the case was meant to centre on issues of free speech, the Court's judgement hardly mentioned them at all. Instead, Kennedy's majority decision focused merely on the state commission's flaws. The exceptions were justices Clarence Thomas and Neil Gorsuch who, although they signed up to the majority opinion, wrote that they would have gone much further and found in favour of Mr Phillips on the grounds of freedom of speech. 'Mr Phillips's cakes are artistic expression worthy of First Amendment protection', Justice Thomas wrote, 'and requiring him to endorse marriages at odds with his faith violated his constitutional rights.'

The reaction was generally welcoming on behalf of those who supported Mr Phillips's rights. The Alliance Defending Freedom, which represented Mr Phillips, said the ruling was a victory for religious liberty. The American Civil Liberties Union, which represented Mr Mullins and Mr Craig, found parts of the judgement both to welcome and to criticise.

When John Roberts took his seat on the Court as chief justice in 2005, he suggested that it would be his practice to seek compromise among the justices so that the majority in cases was as large as possible. Put simply, he was suggesting that he would rather have a 7–2 or a 6–3 decision that took account of a range of views on the Court than a 5–4 decision which reflected the views of mainly just one wing of the Court. 'The rule of law is strengthened when there is greater coherence and agreement about what the law is,' Roberts said in a Georgetown University lecture in 2006. In *Masterpiece Cakeshop* Roberts certainly got widespread agreement, but – many would say – at the expense of coherence.

First Amendment: abortion rights meet religious freedom

There were a number of similar factors between the *Masterpiece Cakeshop* decision and *National Institute of Family and Life Advocates* v *Becera*, for both centred on the extent to which the state can compel people to do and say things that are at odds with their religious beliefs. Do such attempts to compel by the state infringe First Amendment rights? In this case, the Court struck down a California state law that required religiously orientated 'crisis pregnancy centres' to supply women with information about how to end their pregnancies. The state law had required that such centres – run by those who oppose abortion on religious grounds – post notices drawing attention to free or low-cost abortion, contraception and prenatal care that was available to low-income women on publicly funded programmes, and to provide a phone number for such services.

But the centres claimed that the law violated their First Amendment right to free speech by forcing them to display messages that were at odds with their religious beliefs regarding the sanctity of human life. The centres were represented in Court by lawyers provided by the Alliance Defending Freedom (ADF) — the same group that provided legal services to Jack Phillips in the *Masterpiece Cakeshop* case. ADF lawyer Michael Farris stated that 'no-one should be forced by the government to express a message that violates their convictions, especially on deeply divisive subjects such as abortion'.

In its 5–4 judgement, the Court's majority agreed. Writing for the majority, Justice Clarence Thomas — joined by his fellow conservatives Roberts, Alito and Gorsuch, along with Justice Anthony Kennedy — stated that 'California cannot co-opt the licensed facilities to deliver its message [on the availability of abortion] for it.' But perhaps the most interesting part of the majority opinion was stated by Justice Kennedy:

> Governments must not be allowed to force persons to express a message contrary to their deepest convictions. Freedom of speech secures freedom of thought and belief. This law imperils those liberties.

One wonders why the same view was not expressed in such crystal clear terms by the same justice in the case concerning the celebrated wedding cake.

First Amendment: union rights meet freedom of speech

In a significant blow to the United States labour union movement, the Supreme Court ruled (5–4) in *Janus* v *American Federation of State, County and Municipal Employees* that government workers who choose not to join a labour union could not be charged a fee by that union on the pretext that it was to pay for the union's role in collective bargaining. According to the five-person majority — the Court's conservative quartet joined by Justice Kennedy — forcing those workers to finance union activity violated their First Amendment rights. 'We conclude that this arrangement violates the free speech rights of non-members by compelling them to subsidise private speech on matters of substantial public concern', wrote Justice Alito for the majority.

The case was brought by Mark Janus, a child support specialist who worked for the Illinois state government. He sued the union, saying he did not support its positions and therefore should not be forced to pay a fee to support its work. And the decision struck down an Illinois state law that required government employees who chose not to join a union to 'pay their proportionate share of the costs of the collective bargaining process'. More than 20 states had similar legislation on their statute books.

This decision was an example of the Court clearly overruling one of its own decisions made at an earlier date — this one some 40 years ago. In 1977 — when none of the current justices were on the bench — the Court in *Abood* v *Detroit Board of Education* made a distinction between two types of payment made by non-unionised workers to labour unions that represented their profession. In *Abood*, the Court ruled that forcing non-members to pay for a union's political activities violated the First Amendment, but that it was permissible to require non-members to pay for negotiating activities from which all benefited. Writing for the majority now in 2018, Justice Samuel Alito said that such distinctions were untenable and unworkable. '*Abood* was poorly reasoned', wrote Alito, 'and has led to practical problems and abuse.'

The liberal quartet's dissent was authored by Justice Elena Kagan, who accused the majority fivesome of 'subverting all known principles of *stare decisis*' – the legal principle that judges should look to past precedents as a guide wherever possible. (The phrase literally means 'let the decision stand'.) Kagan wrote somewhat waspishly:

> Don't like a decision? Just throw some gratuitous criticisms into a couple of opinions and a few years later point to them as 'special justifications' for overruling a precedent. The majority has overruled *Abood* for no exceptional or special reason, but because it never liked the decision. It has overruled *Abood* because it wanted to.

But Kagan also had concerns that the First Amendment was being dragged into this argument.

> The First Amendment was meant for better things. It was meant not to undermine but to protect democratic governance – including over the role of public sector unions.

That said, one therefore wonders whether Justice Kagan should feel entirely comfortable with the Fourteenth Amendment being dragged into a decision on abortion – *Roe* v *Wade* in 1973. Arguments can play both ways.

Fourth Amendment: the Founding Fathers meet mobile phones

When studying the Supreme Court's power of judicial review, we often say that this gives the Court the power of 'interpretative amendment'. The words remain the same, but their interpretation – by the Supreme Court – changes to bring them up to date in the twenty-first century. Here is a clear example of that happening. When the Founding Fathers drew up the Bill of Rights amendments in the late eighteenth century, they were not much vexed about mobile phones – or 'cell phones' as the Americans call them. Yet in the case of *Carpenter* v *United States*, the Court was having to decide whether or not the state had a right of access to the physical location data held by cell phone companies on their customers without a warrant, or whether such warrantless access would breach people's Fourth Amendment rights of freedom from 'unreasonable searches'.

In another 5–4 decision, Chief Justice John Roberts, writing for the majority, stated that 'we decline to grant the state unrestricted access to a wireless carrier's database of physical location information'. In this decision it was the Chief Justice who joined the Court's liberal quartet to give them the five-member majority, leaving justices Kennedy, Thomas, Alito and Gorsuch as the minority.

The case of *Carpenter* v *United States* arose from a series of armed robberies of stores owned by the electronics firm RadioShack. It was alleged that Timothy Carpenter had planned and orchestrated the raids, and to prove this the police had obtained records of Mr Carpenter's cell phone usage and location. Upon conviction, Carpenter had been sentenced to 116 years in prison. But Carpenter's lawyer claimed that the seizure of his client's phone records had been obtained without a warrant and revealed information of a personal nature about his client's whereabouts. It therefore breached Mr Carpenter's Fourth Amendment rights.

Chief Justice Roberts agreed with Carpenter's lawyer (see Box 3.1). And Roberts also noted how the Court was being asked to relate Fourth Amendment rights — granted in the 1790s — to life in the digital age of the twenty-first century.

Box 3.1 **Extracts from Chief Justice Roberts' majority opinion in *Carpenter* v *United States***

Mapping a cell phone's location over the course of 127 days provides an all-encompassing record of the holder's whereabouts. As with Global Positioning System (GPS) information, the time-stamped data provides an intimate window into a person's life, revealing not only his particular movements, but through them his familial, political, professional, religious and sexual associations...

The question we confront today is how to apply the Fourth Amendment to a new phenomenon: the ability to chronicle a person's past movements through the record of his cell phone signals.

Presidential power: the Trump travel ban

Maybe the most awaited decision of this term was the one concerning President Trump's 'travel ban'. Supreme Court decisions that tell us what presidents can and cannot do are often highly consequential (see Table 3.2). The travel ban case went back to the 2016 presidential campaign, during which (in December 2015) a mass shooting took place in San Bernardino, California, perpetrated by two people of Pakistani descent, who killed 14 people and seriously injured another 22. The two perpetrators had arrived in the United States legally but had then been radicalised online by Islamist terrorist groups based in Saudi Arabia. Immediately after this incident, Donald Trump — then leading the polls in the Republican nomination contest — issued a statement that read:

> Donald J. Trump is calling for a total and complete shutdown of Muslims entering the United States until our country's representatives can figure out what is going on.

The 'Muslim travel ban', as it became known, then featured regularly in Trump campaign speeches during the next year and his core supporters saw delivering it as a litmus test of Trump's authenticity as the president who was going to 'Make America Great Again'.

Table 3.2 Selected recent landmark decisions by the Supreme Court on presidential power

Case	Year	Led to
United States v *Richard Nixon*	1974	Release of the Watergate tapes and Nixon's resignation
Clinton v *Jones*	1997	Investigation into President Clinton's affair with Paula Jones followed by his impeachment
Rasul v *Bush*	2004	Significant changes in President Bush's conduct of his 'war on terror'

Then, exactly a week into his presidency, Trump issued Executive Order 13769 which banned entry of people from seven Muslim-majority countries – Iran, Iraq, Libya, Somalia, Sudan, Syria and Yemen – for at least 90 days, regardless of whether or not they held valid visas. In the text of the order, the President justified the move by making a number of references to the 9/11 attacks on America in 2001. But none of the 9/11 terrorists came from any of these seven countries. Furthermore, noticeably missing from the list was Saudi Arabia – visited by the San Bernardino terrorists, and where Mr Trump has significant business interests. The result of the order was chaos at America's main entry points, most notably the country's largest airports.

Table 3.3 The three Trump travel bans compared

	Travel Ban 1	Travel Ban 2	Travel Ban 3
Date	27 January 2017	6 March 2017	24 September 2017
Outcome	Took effect immediately; blocked by the courts soon after	Blocked initially; in June 2017 the Supreme Court allowed a partial ban	Blocked initially; in December 2017 the Supreme Court allowed it to take effect temporarily
Intended duration	90 days	90 days	Indefinite
Countries affected	Iraq Sudan Syria Iran Libya Somalia Yemen	Sudan Syria Iran Libya Somalia Yemen	Syria Iran Libya Somalia Yemen North Korea Venezuela Chad (later removed)
Refugee provision	Banned for 120 days (Syrians indefinitely) Gave priority to religious minorities facing persecution	Syrians no longer banned indefinitely Removed references to religious minorities	Memo issued in October resumed refugee admissions but instituted a 90-day review for refugees from 11 countries

Source: adapted from www.nytimes, 27 June 2018

Then in March 2017, the President signed a new executive order (13780), removing Iraq from the list of countries to which the travel ban applied. Three days later, this new order was itself the subject of a legal challenge when five states – Washington, Oregon, Hawaii, Massachusetts and Minnesota – filed a challenge in federal court. On 15 March, a federal judge in Hawaii, Derek Watson, issued a temporary restraining order that blocked the new order nationwide, a decision the President described as 'an unprecedented judicial overreach'. It was this case that would end up in the Supreme Court as *Trump* v *Hawaii* but not before the President had issued a third executive order in September 2017 (see Table 3.3).

Having been somewhat ravaged by the lower federal courts, the President was particularly gratified that the Supreme Court upheld his travel ban. By a 5–4 majority, the Court ruled that the president's power to secure the country's borders, delegated by Congress over decades of immigration law making, was not undermined by President Trump's occasionally incendiary statements about the dangers he claimed that Muslims posed to the United States. Needless to say, the President was delighted with the Court's ruling, calling it a 'tremendous victory' (see Box 3.2). The five-member majority was made up of the conservative quartet joined by Justice Kennedy.

> ### Box 3.2 Extract from President Trump's response to the Supreme Court's judgement in *Trump* v *Hawaii*
>
> This ruling is a moment of profound vindication following the months of hysterical commentary from the media and Democratic politicians who refuse to do what it takes to secure our border and our country.

Writing for the dissenting minority, Justice Sonia Sotomayor criticised the President, and quoted many of the anti-Muslim statements he had made both in speeches and on Twitter. 'Let the gravity of these statements sink in', Justice Sotomayor said. She accused her colleagues in the majority of 'unquestioning acceptance' of the President's national security claims, accusing the Court of inconsistency by noting that a stray remark from a Colorado civil rights commissioner expressing hostility to religion had been the basis of a ruling just a few weeks earlier in favour of a Christian baker. 'Those principles should apply equally here', she wrote. 'In both instances, the question is whether a government actor exhibited tolerance and neutrality reaching a decision that affects individuals' fundamental religious freedom.'

Finally, the decision in *Trump* v *Hawaii* was seen by the President's supporters as a clear vindication of Senator Mitch McConnell's strategy of blocking President Obama's nomination to fill the vacancy on the Court created by the death of Justice Scalia. Had President Obama's nominee Judge Merrick Garland been admitted to the Court in 2016 – and not Neil Gorsuch in 2017 – the decision might well have gone the other way. This is another example of how highly consequential presidents' Supreme Court nominations can be.

Questions

1 Summarise the Supreme Court's judgement in *Masterpiece Cakeshop*.
2 Why did the Supreme Court strike down the California state law in the abortion rights case?
3 Summarise the majority and minority arguments in *Janus*.
4 How does the decision in *Carpenter* show the Supreme Court bringing the eighteenth century Constitution into the twenty-first century?
5 Briefly explain the background to the *Trump* v *Hawaii* case.
6 What did the Supreme Court decide in this case?
7 Why was the appointment of Neil Gorsuch to the Court in 2017 so significant in this decision?

Chapter 4

The Supreme Court: overview of the 2017–18 term

What you need to know

- The Supreme Court is the highest court in the USA.
- The Court is made up of nine justices, appointed by the president, for life.
- The Supreme Court has the power of judicial review. This is the power to declare Acts of Congress or actions of the executive branch — or Acts or actions of state governments — unconstitutional, and thereby null and void.
- By this power of judicial review, the Court acts as the umpire of the Constitution and plays a leading role in safeguarding Americans' rights and liberties.

In Chapter 3 we analysed five significant decisions handed down by the Supreme Court in its term which began in October 2017 and ended in June 2018. But these were only five of the 71 decisions handed down by the Court during this term. As Table 4.1 shows, that figure is pretty much par for the course when compared with recent terms. But it is significantly down on the number of judgements handed down a decade ago when, for example, in 2009–10 the Court handed down 86 decisions. This decrease is in line with a stated aim of John Roberts when he joined the Court as chief justice in 2005.

Of these 71 decisions, 56 (79%) were appealed from the federal appellate courts, 8 (11%) from the state appellate courts, and 4 from the court for the District of Columbia, with the remaining 3 cases coming to Court on original jurisdiction.

Unity and division in the Court

Having had high levels of unanimity in three of the last four terms (see Table 4.1), the number of unanimous decisions fell back in this term to the lowest for six years, since the 2008–09 term that saw just 33% of all decisions as unanimous. Unsurprisingly, a fall in unanimity was matched by a rise in 5–4 decisions — up from record lows in the previous two terms, to just over one-quarter of all decisions in 2017–18.

Table 4.1 Total, unanimous and 5–4 decisions, 2012–18

Term:	2012–13	2013–14	2014–15	2015–16	2016–17	2017–18
Number of decisions	78	72	75	76	69	**71**
% which were unanimous	49%	65%	40%	50%	59%	**39%**
% which were 5–4 decisions	29%	14%	26%	5%	10%	**27%**

The 5–4 decisions

One of the most noteworthy facts of the Court's most recent term was the extent to which the Court's conservative wing won the day on so many of the 5–4 decisions. The make-up of the Court in the 2017–18 term according to judicial philosophy is shown in Table 4.2. Of course, these labels are generalisations. They also have the disadvantage of focusing on ideology rather than on judicial philosophy. So it might be more accurate to describe the liberal quartet as loose constructionists and the conservative quartet as strict constructionists. But 'conservative' and 'liberal' are still useful shorthand terms, provided we don't use them pejoratively.

Table 4.2 Make-up of the Supreme Court by ideological position, 2017–18

Liberal wing	Swing justice	Conservative wing
Ruth Bader Ginsburg	Anthony Kennedy	Clarence Thomas
Sonia Sotomayor		Samuel Alito
Stephen Breyer		Neil Gorsuch
Elena Kagan		John Roberts

Of the 19 decisions during the 2017–18 term that were arrived at by 5 votes to 4, 14 of them (74%) featured the conservative quartet joined by Justice Kennedy. Compared with that, not a single decision featured the liberal quartet joined by Justice Kennedy. During the last term when the Court had a full bench of nine justices for the whole term — the 2014–15 term — there were also nineteen 5–4 decisions. But during that term, eight of them (42%) featured the liberal quartet joined by Justice Kennedy, while just five (26%) featured the conservative quartet joined by Justice Kennedy. Figure 4.1 also shows the significant shift between these two terms in the influence that Chief Justice Roberts and Justice Breyer —

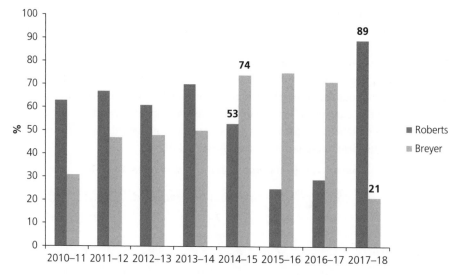

Figure 4.1 Percentage of times in the majority on 5–4 decisions, 2010–18: Roberts and Breyer compared

respectively a conservative and a liberal justice – exerted. Whereas in 2014–15 Justice Breyer was in the majority in 74% of 5–4 decisions, in 2017–18 he was in the majority in only 21% of such decisions. In contrast, between the two terms, Chief Justice Roberts went from being in the majority in 53% of 5–4 decisions to being in the majority in 89% of such decisions.

Figure 4.2 further shows the significantly increased success of the conservative bloc on the Court during the 2017–18 term. With 74% of 5–4 decisions featuring the conservative quartet plus Justice Kennedy, this was significantly higher than had been seen in any of the Court's previous 12 terms – dating back to 2005 when both Chief Justice Roberts and Justice Alito joined the Court. Table 4.3 also shows that it was the four conservative justices plus Justice Kennedy who headed the table of justices most frequently in the majority in 5–4 decisions during this term.

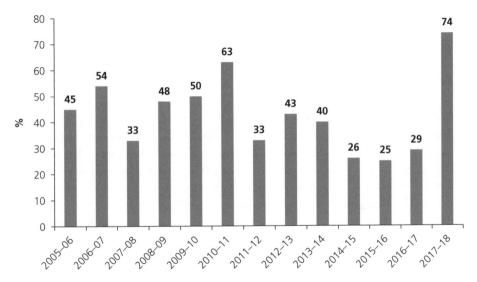

Figure 4.2 Frequency of conservative victories in 5–4 decisions

Table 4.3 Frequency in the majority in 5–4 decisions, 2017–18

Justice	Frequency in majority in 5–4 decisions (%)
John Roberts	89
Anthony Kennedy	84
Neil Gorsuch	84
Clarence Thomas	79
Samuel Alito	79
Ruth Bader Ginsburg	26
Stephen Breyer	21
Sonia Sotomayor	21
Elena Kagan	17

So why this resurgence in conservative influence on the Court in 2017–18? It all seemed to be tied up with the arrival of Justice Neil Gorsuch. Gorsuch had joined the Court in the last few months of the previous term, but by then most of the cases had undergone their oral argument and therefore Justice Gorsuch took no part in decisions regarding them. Gorsuch participated in only 14 of that term's 69 decisions, six of which were unanimous decisions. He took part in only two of that term's seven 5–4 decisions.

But in his first full term, Gorsuch 'turned in the most consequential freshman performance by a member of the Supreme Court in living memory' (Adam Liptak, 'Conservatives in Charge, the Supreme Court Moved Right', *New York Times*, 28 June 2018), supplying a decisive vote in 15 of the 19 cases decided 5–4. In recent terms, Justice Kennedy had been the most often in the majority in 5–4 decisions. But as Table 4.3 shows, in 2017–18 Chief Justice Roberts surpassed him, and Neil Gorsuch tied with him. Thus it was the conservative duo of Roberts and Gorsuch plus the more moderate Kennedy that 'occupied the ideological space at the Court's centre, which had for years been home to Justice Kennedy by himself' (Liptak).

Identical twins and odd couples

From looking at patterns of agreement and disagreement between the justices, one can also discern subtle shifts taking place on the Court. Whereas for the previous two terms the two justices most often in agreement were Anthony Kennedy and Obama appointee Elena Kagan, this term it was two on the liberal wing of the Court – Ginsburg and Sotomayor – who were the Court's identical twins, agreeing on 86% of all decisions (see Table 4.4). Kennedy and Kagan, who had previously been so close, certainly parted company in this term. Having agreed on 88% of cases in 2016–17, they agreed on only 62% of cases in 2017–18.

Table 4.4 Agreement and disagreement between justices, 2012–18

Term:	2012–13	2013–14	2014–15	2015–16	2016–17	2017–18
Justices most in agreement	Ginsburg Kagan	Thomas Alito	Breyer Ginsburg	Kennedy Kagan	Kennedy Kagan	Ginsburg Sotomayor
Justices most in disagreement	Alito Ginsburg	Alito Sotomayor	Thomas Sotomayor	Thomas Ginsburg	Thomas Ginsburg	Alito Sotomayor

Meanwhile, in the odd couples contest, Alito and Sotomayor seemed to re-establish themselves at the Court's ideological ends, agreeing on only 12% of non-unanimous cases.

Differences in approach

Some justices work quicker than others, as shown in Figure 4.3. The average number of days between oral argument of a case and the publication of its majority opinion was 109 days – well up on the average of 92 days in the previous term. But whereas Justice Ginsburg averaged just 74 days, Chief Justice Roberts took on average 125 days – almost two months longer.

The justices also differ quite widely in how they operate on the bench at oral argument. Put simply, some talk more than others. Whereas Justice Thomas – as usual – asked no questions at all at oral argument, Justice Sotomayor asked an average of 24, and Justice Breyer an average of 21 (see Table 4.5). On the other hand, although Justice Kennedy was often regarded by lawyers appearing before the Court as potentially the most important person to address – because of his position in the ideological centre of the Court – he was, other than Thomas, the least forthcoming when it came to questioning.

For the sixth consecutive term, Justice Ginsburg was the most frequent asker of the first question at oral argument (see Table 4.6), doing so in over half the cases. However, although the 85-year-old justice is usually first off the mark when it comes to questions, Table 4.5 shows that she asks, on average, fewer questions than all her colleagues except Justice Kennedy and the ever-silent Justice Thomas.

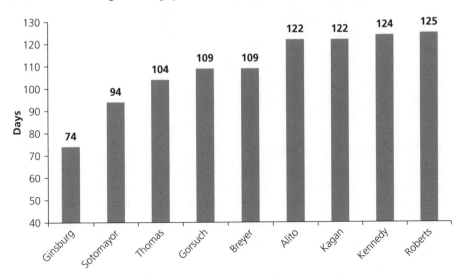

Figure 4.3 Days between oral argument and majority opinion

Table 4.5 Average number of questions per oral argument

Justice	Average
Sotomayor	24
Breyer	21
Roberts	16
Gorsuch	15
Kagan	14
Alito	12
Ginsburg	10
Kennedy	9
Thomas	0

Table 4.6 Frequency as the first questioner at oral argument

Justice	Frequency (%)
Ginsburg	54
Sotomayor	17
Kennedy	13
Roberts	10
Kagan	3
Gorsuch	2
Alito	2
Thomas	0
Breyer	0

So whose Court is it anyway?

Since the retirement of Justice Sandra Day O'Connor in 2005, the United States Supreme Court has most accurately been described as 'the Kennedy Court'. Justice Kennedy, prizing his place at its centre, has voted this way and that way, seemingly always trying to put together a five-member majority, whether with conservatives or liberals. But in this his last term on the Court, Kennedy already seemed to have lost his place at the Court's pivotal centre, ceding that to Chief Justice Roberts. It was Roberts, after all, who was the justice most frequently in the majority – in all cases, in non-unanimous cases and in 5–4 cases.

It seems likely that, with Anthony Kennedy now to be replaced by someone much more predictably conservative, the new Court's conservative quartet will be Thomas, Alito, Gorsuch and Kavanaugh – Kennedy's replacement – with Chief Justice Roberts becoming the new swing justice. 'Should Roberts become the median justice, the Court could move well to the right, taking its place as the most conservative court in modern history', commented Professor Lee Epstein of

Washington University in St Louis. In this term that finished in June 2018, Chief Justice Roberts seemed to be moving towards the Court's centre. 'This gave us a preview of what the Supreme Court would be like if Chief Justice Roberts were to become the swing vote', stated Leah Litman, a law professor at the University of California, Irvine. 'Progressives will lose, and they will lose a lot.' Time will tell.

Questions

1 Analyse the data presented in Table 4.1.
2 What was significant about the 5–4 decisions in this term?
3 Explain which ideological wing of the Court Roberts and Breyer come from, and then analyse the data presented in Figures 4.1 and 4.2, and Table 4.3.
4 What reason does the author suggest for the resurgence in conservative influence on the Court in 2017–18?
5 What do Figure 4.3 and Tables 4.5 and 4.6 tell us about the different ways in which the justices work?
6 How might the role of Chief Justice Roberts change in the coming years? What effect would that have on the Court as a whole?

The Trump presidency after two years

Setting the scene

During the first week of September, 2018, in the twentieth month of the Trump presidency, readers of the *New York Times* were treated to the following critique of the incumbent president and his administration:

> From the White House to the executive branch departments and agencies, senior officials will privately admit their daily disbelief at the Commander-in-Chief's comments and actions. Most are working to insulate their operations from his whims. Meetings with him veer off topic and off the rails. He engages in repetitive rants, and his impulsiveness results in half-baked, ill-informed and occasionally reckless decisions that have to be walked back.

At first glance, such comments might not be overly surprising. After all, the *Times* is not known for its support for Republican presidents — whether named Reagan, Bush or Trump. And many readers would not be surprised were such comments to be made by a *Times* editorialist or by a Democratic Party politician or supporter. But at the bottom of this commentary were the words, 'The writer is a senior official in the Trump administration.' In a piece of commentary running to less than 1,000 words, the President was described as 'misguided', 'amoral', 'impetuous', 'petty', 'ineffective' and 'erratic'. Yes, one might have read similar comments on past presidents — after they had left office, by disgruntled officials who had either been sacked or claimed they had heard such remarks, second-hand. But for a serving 'senior official' to make such a verbal demolition of a sitting president really was extraordinary.

The danger is that, if you are coming to study the American presidency for the first time in the era of President Trump, you might think that this is how things normally work and what things normally look like. But the first thing to learn is that there is nothing normal about the Trump presidency. It is all abnormal — in its chaos, in its tone, in its disregard of the norms of democratic working and accountability.

The Trump White House

The first thing that strikes you about the Trump White House is its instability. Even before all the positions in the new administration were filled, senior officials were either resigning or being fired. Even by halfway through Trump's second year in office, some 15 senior members of the White House had either been fired or resigned (see Table 5.1). These included two national security advisers (NSAs), two deputy NSAs, two communications directors, Press Secretary Sean Spicer and White House Chief of Staff Reince Priebus. When compared with recent administrations, this is a significantly higher rate of turnover than one would normally expect. In his controversial book on the Trump White House, Michael Wolff (*Fire and Fury: Inside the Trump White House*, 2018) wrote:

> In most White Houses, policy and action flow down [from the president], with staff trying to implement what the president wants. In the Trump White House, policy making flowed up. It was a process of suggesting, in throw-it-against-the-wall-style, what the president might want, and hoping he might then think he had thought of this himself.

He quoted White House Deputy Chief of Staff Katie Walsh as saying: it was 'like trying to figure out what a child wants'. Ms Walsh lasted only two months in post before she resigned, returning to work at the Republican National Committee.

Table 5.1 Selected resignations and firings from the Trump White House

Date resigned/fired	Name	Position
13 February **2017**	Michael Flynn	National Security Adviser
30 March	Katie Walsh	Deputy Chief of Staff
19 May	K.T. McFarland	Deputy National Security Adviser
21 July	Sean Spicer	White House Press Secretary
31 July	Reince Priebus	White House Chief of Staff
	Anthony Scaramucci	White House Director of Communications
18 August	Steve Bannon	White House Strategist
25 August	Sebastian Gorka	Deputy Assistant to the President
7 February **2018**	Rob Porter	White House Staff Secretary
13 March	Gary Cohn	Director of National Economic Council
29 March	Hope Hicks	White House Director of Communications
9 April	H.R. McMaster	National Security Adviser
11 May	Rob Joyce	Homeland Security Adviser
15 May	Ricky Waddell	Deputy National Security Adviser
20 July	Marc Short	Director of Legislative Affairs

During the Reagan administration, critics worried that the President seemed to want everything on one side of A4. Similar comments came out of the White House during the George W. Bush administration. But according to White House sources, Trump doesn't really relate to printed material at all. 'If it was in print, it might as well not exist,' commented one White House aide. Trump, according to another source, is 'postliterate' – all television and Twitter, where his misspellings proved a frequent source of amusement or amazement, depending on one's point of view.

According to Wolff's sources, not only does Trump not read, he doesn't listen either. He much prefers to be the person doing the talking – unless the person

talking is paying him a compliment. Trump has a very high opinion of his own abilities coupled with a short attention span — not a great twosome for someone sitting behind the Oval Office desk, and for someone who tweets about the size and power of his nuclear button (see Box 5.1). As Uri Friedman wrote a few days after this tweet in his column in the *Atlantic* magazine ('The Terrifying Truth of Trump's "Nuclear Button" Tweet'):

> Setting aside the technicalities of Donald Trump's boast (he has a briefcase, not a button), the Commander-in-Chief was casually sounding off on social media about war with the world's deadliest weapons…He was daring Kim [Jong Un] to prove that his 'nuclear button' works by, for example, testing a missile with a live nuclear weapon over the Pacific Ocean.

Box 5.1 Tweet written by President Trump, 3 January 2018

North Korean leader Kim Jong Un just stated that the 'Nuclear Button is on his desk at all times.' Will someone from his depleted and food starved regime please inform him that I too have a Nuclear Button, but it is much bigger & more powerful one than his, and my Button works!

Source: @realDonaldTrump, accessed 19 September 2018

All this has engendered a feeling of crisis and instability in the Trump White House. Maybe Trump coming after Barack Obama — sometimes referred to as 'No Drama Obama' — hasn't helped him. Most White Houses have had their crises — just not at the frequency or severity we have seen thus far in the White House of President Trump.

The Trump cabinet

The first thing that strikes you about the Trump cabinet is also its instability. George W. Bush made just one change of personnel in his cabinet during his first two years. Barack Obama made none. Obama was well into his third year before his first cabinet personnel change took place. But Trump's second year was not halfway through before four of his original cabinet had resigned, been fired or moved. According to Tamara Keith of National Public Radio, no elected first-term president in the past 100 years has had this much turnover this early in his presidency.

Box 5.2 Trump tweets on Attorney General Jeff Sessions

- 'Attorney General Jeff Sessions has taken a VERY weak position on Hillary Clinton crimes and Intel leakers!' (25 July 2017)
- 'The Russian Witch Hunt continues, all because Jeff Sessions didn't tell me he was going to recuse himself. I would have quickly picked someone else.' (5 June 2018)
- 'Two long running, Obama era, investigations of two very popular Republican Congressmen were brought to a well publicized charge, just ahead of the Mid-Terms, by the Jeff Sessions Justice Department. Two easy wins now in doubt because there is not enough time. Good job Jeff…' (3 September 2018)

In July of Trump's first year, Health and Human Services Secretary Tom Price resigned and Homeland Security Secretary John Kelly was moved to be White House chief of staff. Then in March of 2018, both Secretary of State Rex Tillerson and Veterans Affairs Secretary David Shulkin were fired – Tillerson becoming the first cabinet secretary to be fired by a tweet! Cabinet chairs also changed occupancy when Mike Pompeo was switched from the CIA to the State Department to replace Tillerson and when Scott Pruitt resigned as the administrator of the Environmental Protection Agency. Added to that, 2018 saw a chorus of criticism and complaint by Trump directed at his attorney general, Jeff Sessions, who was fired the day after the midterm elections (see Box 5.2).

Table 5.2 Personnel changes in Donald Trump's cabinet, 2017–18

Post	Original appointee	Replacement appointee
Secretary of Health and Human Services	Tom Price	Alex Azar
Secretary of Homeland Security	John Kelly	Kirstjen Nielsen
Secretary of State	Rex Tillerson	Mike Pompeo
Secretary of Veterans Affairs	David Shulkin	Robert Wilkie
Attorney General	Jeff Sessions	Matthew Whitaker (Acting)

The second thing that strikes you about the Trump cabinet is the frequency with which it meets with the President in formal cabinet meetings at the White House. During the four years of his first term in office, President Obama held just 16 full cabinet meetings – five in the first year, four each in his second and third years, and just three in the fourth year. By contrast, Trump held his sixteenth cabinet meeting on 16 August 2018 – less than 17 months into his presidency. This is a greater frequency than any president since President Reagan. Trump also held a cabinet weekend away at Camp David on 5–7 January 2018.

Table 5.3 Trump cabinet meetings, 2017–18

	2017		2018
1	13 March	10	10 January
2	12 June	11	8 March
3	31 July	12	9 April
4	9 September	13	9 May
5	15 October	14	21 June
6	1 November	15	18 July
7	20 November	16	16 August
8	6 December	17	17 October
9	20 December	18	1 November

The impetus behind the frequent and regular cabinet meetings appears to have been White House Chief of Staff John Kelly, who took over from Trump's first chief of staff Reince Priebus on 31 July 2017. Up to that point, the Trump cabinet had met only twice in over six months. Since then, it has met pretty much every four weeks (see Table 5.3). Upon taking office, Kelly announced that there would from then on be regular cabinet meetings with 'focused agendas' (see Table 5.4). The trouble with 'focused agendas' at cabinet meetings in a system where there is no collective responsibility is that cabinet officers have little or nothing to say on issues outside their own policy areas. One wonders, for example, what the secretaries of state and defense made of the 16 October 2017 meeting.

Table 5.4 Agenda items at selected Trump cabinet meetings, 2017–18

Cabinet meeting	Agenda items included:
16 October **2017**	• domestic policy issues • unemployment • prescription drug prices
1 November	• terrorist attack in New York City • immigration • tax cuts
20 November	• report on President's 12-day trip to Asia • tax plan
6 December	• situation in North Korea • update on national security • job creation
9 April **2018**	• trade negotiations with China • South Korea deal • opioid crisis
18 July	• the economy • jobs • workforce training

Cabinet meetings typically fulfil a number of different functions. The president can use them, for example, to exchange information, debate policies, present 'big picture' items and monitor legislation in Congress. Meetings also give cabinet officers the chance to resolve inter-departmental disputes and speak with the president. But as we commented in the 2018 edition of this publication, in the Trump administration the cabinet meeting seems to have added another function – that of presidential ego-stroking. This comes in two forms: either the President – usually at the start of the meeting when selected members of the press are still in attendance – makes fulsome claims about the success of his administration (see Box 5.3); or individual cabinet members sing the President's praises. As Julie Hirschfeld Davis wrote in the *New York Times* ('Once Dry Discussions, Cabinet Meetings Are Now Part of the Trump Show', 16 August 2018): 'What was once considered a dry policy discussion among restrained public servants has turned into a kind of West Wing performance art, featuring a president prone to exaggeration and his advisers taking turns to praise him and his policies.'

Box 5.3 **Extract from President Trump's statement at the start of the cabinet meeting, 10 January 2018**

We've set a new record on reducing regulations and all forms of stopping growth and stopping jobs that were crippling America's economy. Again, the records we've set — nobody's come close. And the number of regulations we've cut is also a record in our country's history...We've passed the largest tax cut and reform in American history...We're also making America safe again. Yesterday we had a bipartisan meeting with House members and senators on immigration reform — something they've been talking about for many, many years, but we brought them together in this room, and it was a tremendous meeting. Actually, it was reported as incredibly good, and my performance — you know some of them called it a performance, I consider it work — but got great reviews by everybody other than two [TV] networks who were phenomenal for about two hours, and after that they were called by their bosses, and then they said, 'Oh, wait a minute...'. And fortunately lots of those [TV] anchors sent us letters saying that was one of the greatest meetings they'd ever witnessed...

Source: transcribed from Fox News video posted on YouTube

This again is government as reality television with the focus always on the star of the show. After all, Trump did host *The Apprentice* on America's NBC channel between 2004 and 2015. At times, it can seem as if he sees his administration as a kind of extension of that TV success.

Trump and the Republican Party

Ever since June 2015, when Donald Trump glided down the golden escalator into the lobby of Trump Tower in New York City and declared, 'I am officially running for president of the United States', there have been not one, but two Republican parties. On the one hand, there is what one might call the establishment Republican Party. This is the party to which both former presidents George Bush belong, along with the Republican Party leadership in Congress, the Republican National Committee, and most elected Republican members of Congress and state governments — though there are some exceptions, especially in the House of Representatives. This is the party of former Republican presidential candidates — of the late John McCain and of Mitt Romney. This party is internationalist, wants to reach out to Latino and Hispanic voters, is in favour of free trade and views the current Russian leadership with huge scepticism, believing both that they have tried to interfere in American elections in the past, and that they continue to do so.

But running parallel with this party is what one might call the insurgent Republican Party — the party of Donald Trump. When Trump won the presidential nomination of the Republican Party in the summer of 2016, in effect he made a hostile takeover of the party that had existed for one-and-a-half centuries – a party that traces its roots back to Abraham Lincoln. The power base of Trump's Republican Party is not in Washington DC, it's not in Congress – it's at the grassroots level of the so-called 'red states' that voted for Trump in 2016. These states are mainly in the South, the Midwest, the Mountain states from Idaho to the Dakotas, and the old Rust Belt states. Trump's Republican Party is made up not of senators, congressmen, state governors and city mayors, but of ordinary voters – mostly men – who live in the small towns and rural parts of the United States, folk who probably didn't get an education past high school and are overwhelmingly white and middle-aged or older. Just look at the faces in the crowds at Trump rallies.

It would not be an exaggeration to say that the insurgent Republican Party views itself as being at war not only with the Democrats – the party of 'crooked Hillary [Clinton]' and 'loser Nancy [Pelosi]' – but with establishment Republicans. And Trump often feels the same. On the day that I'm writing this chapter, the President is venting his wrath on Twitter about a spending bill passed by the *Republican-* controlled House of Representatives.

> I want to know, where is the money for Border Security and the WALL in this ridiculous Spending Bill, and where will it come from after the Midterms? Dems are obstructing Law Enforcement and Border Security. REPUBLICANS MUST FINALLY GET TOUGH!

In Chapter 1, we saw how these two manifestations of the Republican Party came to the surface during the Republican congressional primaries, with Trump openly endorsing some challengers against incumbent Republicans in the primaries. That said, for the time being at least, most establishment Republicans – including the party leadership in Congress – have been prepared to go along with the President and have avoided criticising him even for his more outlandish comments and actions. What the medium- and long-term effects of Trump will be for the Republican Party is presently difficult to assess.

Trump and the federal judiciary

One reason why many conservatives – both politicians and voters – continue to support Donald Trump despite his erratic and controversial behaviour is that they want a president who will appoint 'conservative' judges to the federal courts. These lifetime appointments are among the most significant appointments that a president makes. When President Trump arrived into the Oval Office in January 2017 he inherited more than 100 federal judicial vacancies. This was partly because the Senate Republicans had deliberately kept many vacancies unfilled during the final months of President Obama's second term. One of them was, of course, to the Supreme Court. But there were numerous vacancies in the federal appeal courts, sometimes referred to as the circuit courts – the courts immediately below the Supreme Court. Only a small fraction of cases will ever make it all the way to the Supreme Court; it is in the federal appeal courts that most cases are decided. What is more, most Supreme Court justices are recruited from the ranks of the appeal court judges. So although these judicial nominations get almost no coverage in the media, they are highly significant.

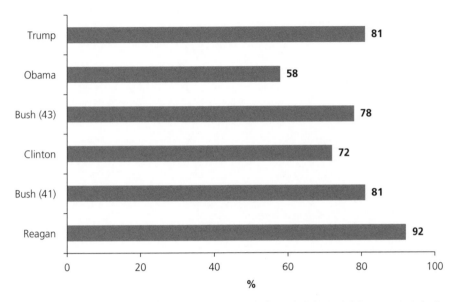

Figure 5.1 Percentage of federal appeal court judges appointed who were male: by presidency, 1981–2018

By the autumn of 2018, President Trump – with the help of a Republican-controlled Senate – had already placed 26 new judges on the federal appeals bench, more than any other president had achieved in his first two years in office. Trump's appeal court appointees are noteworthy in four respects. First, they are on average more male than those appointed by any of his three immediate predecessors (see Figure 5.1). Second, they are more white than those appointed by any of his four immediate predecessors (see Figure 5.2). Having said that, Trump's appointments are not all that out of line in terms of gender and race when compared with his *Republican* predecessors – Bush (43), Bush (41) and Reagan. Third, whereas the average age of nominees to these courts by previous presidents has been around 50, Trump's appointees are younger. That means that these judges, who will serve for life, will shape the legal landscape for decades to come.

But fourth, another characteristic of these new judges is their ideological similarity. 'We're going to have great judges – conservatives – all picked by the Federalist Society,' promised candidate Donald Trump in June 2016. And this is one campaign promise on which President Trump has certainly delivered. Indeed, he's gone one better. For nearly half of his judicial nominees have not just been picked by, but are members of, the Federalist Society – an influential organisation of some 65,000 conservative lawyers and scholars. Chris Kang, a lawyer who worked in the Obama White House, where he oversaw judicial nominations for four years, commented recently: 'I'm sure that some of these people, any Republican president would pick. But it's remarkable how clear they are being about where this is being sourced. It's so brazen.' And Kristine Lucius, executive vice president of the Leadership Conference on Civil and Human Rights, warned: 'These folks are on a mission. Their mission is not neutrality, their mission is not independence, their mission is [a conservative] takeover.'

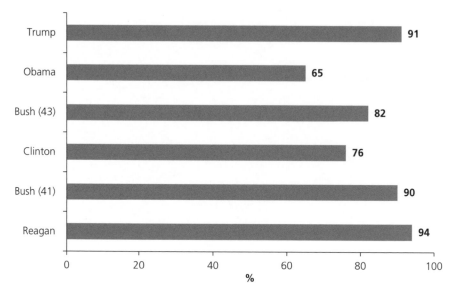

Figure 5.2 Percentage of federal appeal court judges appointed who were white: by presidency, 1981–2018

Trump's legal jeopardy

As the second year closes on the Trump presidency, the President faces legal jeopardy on assorted fronts. These include law suits that were on-going at the time of writing and/or are likely to take shape in the coming months. They involve:

- Stormy Daniels — a pornographic film actress, regarding a non-disclosure agreement signed by her, Donald Trump and Trump's personal lawyer Michael Cohen. Cohen has now pleaded guilty to eight charges in federal court, one charge relating to the Daniels–Trump matter.
- Karen McDougal — a model and actress who alleges an affair with Trump (2006–07). The *National Enquirer* magazine paid McDougall $150,000 for exclusive rights to her story but never published it. McDougal alleges the payment was made merely to kill off damaging stories about Trump during the 2016 election campaign.
- *District of Columbia and Maryland* v *Trump* and *Blumenthal* v *Trump* — cases in which it is alleged that President Trump has violated the Foreign Emoluments Clause of Article I, Section 9 of the Constitution by accepting gifts from foreign governments through revenues at various Trump properties, such as the Trump International Hotel in Washington DC.
- Possible violation of tax laws by the Donald J. Trump Foundation during the 2016 election campaign.
- The Special Counsel's investigation into Russian interference in the 2016 election campaign 'and any matters that arose or may arise from the investigation'.

For sure, other recent presidents — most notably Bill Clinton — faced a number of legal challenges while in office, including a special counsel investigation. What seems different this time around is the number of them, the potential seriousness of some of them, and the fact that they have appeared so early in the President's first term.

Trump and public opinion

On 23 January 2016, then candidate Donald Trump told a campaign rally in Iowa, 'I could stand in the middle of Fifth Avenue and shoot somebody and I wouldn't lose voters.' While probably not literally true, Trump seems to be correct in believing that he has a solid core of support who actually approve of his unconventional presidency and politics. This group of 'Trumpeteers' seems to represent between 30 and 35% of the electorate. This explains why the bottom has yet to fall out of Trump's approval ratings (see Figure 5.3). But it's probably equally true that he could stand in the middle of Fifth Avenue and hand out packets of hundred-dollar bills and – among certain groups of people – he wouldn't *gain* voters. And that's why Trump has yet to have a quarterly approval average above 45% – 24 percentage points below Obama's highest quarterly approval average of 69% (see Figure 5.4).

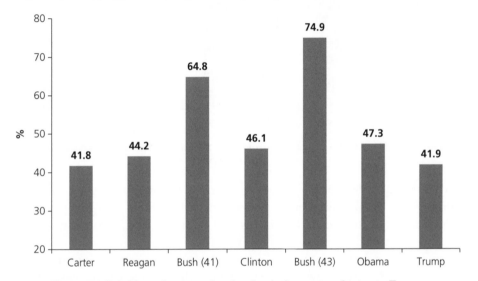

Figure 5.3 Presidents' approval rating in sixth quarter: Carter to Trump

True, Figure 5.3 shows Trumps sixth quarter (20 April–19 July 2018) average little different from that of presidents Jimmy Carter, Ronald Reagan, Bill Clinton or Barack Obama. But as Figure 5.4 shows, those four presidents had already shown their ability to attract the approval of between 58% (Bill Clinton) and 75% (Jimmy Carter) of voters. In contrast, Trump's highest approval rating thus far in his presidency is just 45%.

Of course, we've been writing about 'the partisan presidency' for some years now. There was a time when Democrat-inclined voters would still be persuadable that a Republican president was doing a good job, and Republican voters were in the same way persuadable about Democrat presidents. Republican Gerald Ford had a 36% approval among Democrats; Democrat Jimmy Carter had a 30% approval among Republicans. But during the era of Bill Clinton and George W. Bush things changed. Respectively, they had 27% and 23% approval ratings from the opposing party's supporters. Then for Democrat Barack Obama, Republican voters gave him a 14% approval rating. Even at the very start of his presidency, Democrats gave Donald

Trump a 13% approval rating. By September 2018, the Gallup poll measured Trump's approval rating among Democrats at just 6%. This makes it increasingly difficult for modern-day presidents to win high levels of approval among all Americans. For Trump, it looks well-nigh impossible.

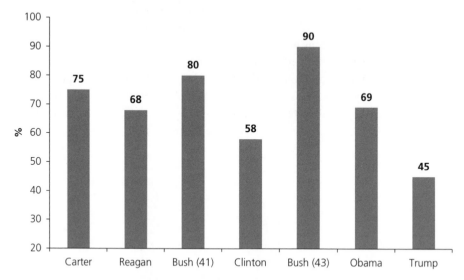

Figure 5.4 President's highest approval rating (Gallup) in first two years: Carter to Trump

What this all means for the future of the Trump presidency is, as yet, too early to say. Will Trump, like Ronald Reagan and Bill Clinton, turn things around significantly in the second half of his first term and then, facing a weak(ish) opponent, stroll to an easy re-election? Will Trump become ensnared in any of the legal traps that still potentially lie in his path? Will the economy go pear-shaped and Trump's core supporters turn against him? The only thing that seems certain is that the next two years will be uncertain.

Questions

1 In what ways has 'instability' been seen in the Trump White House?
2 What do Boxes 5.1 and 5.2 tell us about the problematic nature of Trump's tweeting?
3 What has been unusual about the turnover in the Trump cabinet?
4 What has been unusual about the frequency of Trump cabinet meetings?
5 Give two examples of 'presidential ego-stroking' in Trump cabinet meetings.
6 In what ways does the 'establishment Republican Party' differ from the 'insurgent Republican Party'?
7 How and to what extent has President Trump managed to keep his campaign promises about the make-up of the federal judiciary?
8 Give three examples of possible legal jeopardy facing President Trump.
9 What do Figures 6.3 and 6.4 tell us about President Trump's approval rating compared with those of his immediate predecessors?
10 Why is it difficult for presidents to gain high approval ratings these days?

Chapter 6

Making the presidency great again

Ranking presidents

In the words of Alexander Hamilton, the American people 'build lasting monuments of their gratitude' for certain presidents, but not others. Only a few presidents have been deemed worthy of such enduring respect and reverence as to have the federal capital — Washington DC — graced with a monument to them. A 60-year period between the end of the Civil War and the Second World War saw the erection of the Washington Monument (completed in 1888), the Lincoln Memorial (1922) and the Jefferson Memorial (1943) — memorialising respectively America's first, third and sixteenth presidents. Two have been added in my lifetime: the Theodore Roosevelt Island National Memorial (1967) and the Franklin D. Roosevelt Memorial 30 years later, but neither is quite on the same grand scale as the other three.

Great presidents not only have monuments in the nation's capital but become the subject of numerous biographies, novels, films and TV docudramas. Cities, towns, roads, bridges, buildings and babies are named after them. George Washington alone has a state, 31 counties, 25 towns and cities — including the federal capital where you'll also find Washington Circle, and the George Washington Memorial Parkway. And then there's Mount Rushmore in South Dakota memorialising the great four — Washington, Jefferson, Lincoln and Teddy Roosevelt. Great presidents are on stamps and bank notes. They have their own federal holidays. Even when they are reviled, they are spoken of with awe. It's almost as if these presidents occupied a different position, lived on a different political plane from other incumbents of the presidential office, many of whom are forgotten almost as soon as they leave office.

American academics love to rank their presidents: great, near great, high average…and all the way down to failure. Other ranks just do a straight 1 to 43 (or whatever) rather like sports teams being ranked for the season. On the surface it might appear like a harmless parlour game. But what lies behind it is an undoubted national admiration for, even an addiction to, the 'great leader'. And with Donald Trump promising to 'make America great again' it seems like a good time to see whether it's time to 'make the presidency great again'.

So let's begin by looking at some of the recent polls of presidential greatness. And in case you think this is all very straightforward, it isn't. The first thing we need to realise is that when it comes to questions of presidential greatness, the answers you get depend on two things: they depend on *what* you ask, and on *who* you ask.

Table 6.1 Opinion poll evidence on presidential standings

Public opinion polls	
Rasmussen (2007): favourable/unfavourable	**Gallup (2011): greatest**
1 George Washington	1 Ronald Reagan
2 Abraham Lincoln	2 Abraham Lincoln
3 Thomas Jefferson	3 Bill Clinton
4 Theodore Roosevelt	4 John Kennedy
5 Franklin D. Roosevelt	5 George Washington
6 John Kennedy	6 Franklin D. Roosevelt
7 John Adams	7 Theodore Roosevelt
8 James Madison	8 Harry Truman
9 Ronald Reagan	9 George W. Bush
10 Dwight Eisenhower	10 Thomas Jefferson

In Table 6.1 we have the results of two opinion polls – in other words, ordinary Americans were asked. But they were asked different questions. The Rasmussen poll asked respondents to judge presidents according to favourability, while the Gallup poll asked for a judgement on greatness – whatever that is. And although there are some similarities, there are also stark differences. So, for example, Ronald Reagan came ninth in favourability, but first in greatness – where favourability refers to their rating among ordinary people at the time and greatness refers to their standing in history sometime later. Bill Clinton came third in greatness, but failed to make the top ten in favourability. (He actually came twentieth.)

In Table 6.2, academic scholars on the presidency were asked for their rankings – but this survey distinguished between scholars who identified themselves as

Table 6.2 Scholars' poll evidence on presidential standings: liberals and conservatives compared

Scholars' polls	
'Liberal' scholars	**'Conservative' scholars**
1 George Washington	1 George Washington
2 Abraham Lincoln	2 Abraham Lincoln
3 Franklin D. Roosevelt	3 Thomas Jefferson
4 Thomas Jefferson	4 Andrew Jackson
5 Andrew Jackson	5 Ronald Reagan (26)
6 James Polk (16)	6 Theodore Roosevelt
7 Theodore Roosevelt	7 Franklin D. Roosevelt
8 Woodrow Wilson (28)	8 Dwight Eisenhower (13)
9 Harry Truman (15)	9 John Adams (16)
10 James Monroe (17)	10 John Quincy Adams (18)

Figures in brackets indicate where that president was ranked in the opposite poll.

politically liberal and those identifying as politically conservative. Although the two groups picked a very similar top four, conservatives demoted FDR to seventh, while liberals placed Ronald Reagan – ranked fifth by conservatives – at number 26. Likewise, while liberals placed Woodrow Wilson in eighth spot, conservatives demoted him to well down the second half of the rankings at number 28.

The most recent polling on presidential greatness came in a C-SPAN poll of presidential historians in 2017. The academics were asked to judge presidents from Washington to Obama according to ten criteria, including such matters as public persuasion, crisis leadership, economic management, moral authority and relations with Congress. Their overall rankings are shown in Table 6.3.

Table 6.3 Historians' poll of presidential greatness

C-SPAN (2017) poll of presidential historians	
1 Abraham Lincoln	23 Grover Cleveland
2 George Washington*	24 William Howard Taft
3 Franklin D. Roosevelt*	**25 Gerald Ford**
4 Theodore Roosevelt	**26 Jimmy Carter**
5 Dwight Eisenhower*	27 Calvin Coolidge
6 Harry Truman	**28 Richard Nixon**
7 Thomas Jefferson*	29 James Garfield
8 John Kennedy	30 Benjamin Harrison
9 Ronald Reagan*	31 Zachary Taylor
10 Lyndon Johnson	32 Rutherford Hayes
11 Woodrow Wilson*	**33 George W. Bush***
12 Barack Obama*	34 Martin Van Buren
13 James Monroe*	35 Chester Arthur
14 James Polk	36 Herbert Hoover
15 Bill Clinton*	37 Millard Fillmore
16 William McKinley	38 William Harrison
17 James Madison*	39 John Tyler
18 Andrew Jackson*	40 Warren Harding
19 John Adams	41 Franklin Pierce
20 George H.W. Bush	42 Andrew Johnson
21 John Quincy Adams	43 James Buchanan
22 Ulysses Grant*	

Bold = presidents from 1961 to 2016
* = served two full consecutive terms

Having set that background, we are now going to address three questions about presidential greatness:

1 What factors can lead to presidential greatness?
2 Should we still be talking of presidential greatness?
3 Why might the days of presidential greatness be over?

What factors can lead to presidential greatness?

Serving two full consecutive terms

A number of these factors were identified by the presidential historians in putting together their 2017 poll for C-SPAN. But before we consider those, let's add one of our own. From studying Table 6.3, it seems very clear that presidents who serve two full consecutive terms are far more likely to be rated as 'great' than those who serve only one. Of the 13 presidents who have served two full consecutive terms, 12 are in the top half of the table. Only George W. Bush is in the lower half. Between them, their average position in the table is twelfth. Of the 15 presidents who served only one full term, James Polk was the highest placed (14), and between them their average position was thirtieth.

Public persuasion

Even in an era of partisanship, when both politicians and ordinary voters are less open to presidential persuasion than they used to be, Professor Neustadt's claim that 'presidential power is the power to persuade' is probably still pretty much on the money. Four post-war presidents feature in the top ten in this category in the C-SPAN poll – Reagan (5), Kennedy (6), Clinton (9) and Obama (10). Two modern-day presidents feature in the bottom ten of this category – Ford (34) and Carter (35).

And you don't have to take a partisan position to be able to appreciate the difference between the persuasive skills of Ronald Reagan and Gerald Ford, or of John Kennedy and Jimmy Carter. The skill of public persuasion is also linked to oratorical skills – skills that were clearly present in bucketfuls with Reagan and Kennedy, and were equally clearly absent on most occasions with Ford and Carter. Presidential greatness is a closer relative to 'a shining city on a hill' (Reagan) or 'ask not what your country can do for you...' (Kennedy) than to Ford and Carter's often fumbled and bumbled public utterances.

Crisis leadership

Two days after the 9/11 attacks on New York and Washington, Chris Matthews, the host of MSNBC's *Hardball*, praised what he saw as George W. Bush's good fortune. This is what Matthews said:

> Lucky though he was, Bill Clinton never had a shot at greatness. He could lower the jobless rate, balance the budget, and console us after the Oklahoma City bombing. But he never got the opportunity George W. Bush was given: the historic chance to lead. Our American spirit, power and enterprise now stand ready for orders. Only the president can give them.

Not, of course, that national crisis always gives birth to great leaders. Few would put George W. Bush in that category – certainly the C-SPAN historians did not – and further afield neither the fall of the Soviet Union nor the Arab Spring have brought many glowing examples of great leaders in the mould of a George Washington or an Abraham Lincoln.

But that said, it is worthy of note that a number of the top ten greats in Table 6.3 had very profound opportunities to exhibit the quality of crisis leadership – and certainly that was true of the top three with the Civil War (Lincoln), the War of Independence and its aftermath (Washington) and the Second World War (FDR). Truman (6) had the Cold War and Kennedy (8) the Cuba Missile Crisis. And Reagan (9) showed greatness in his 'Mr Gorbachev, tear down this wall' speech at the Brandenburg Gate in 1987.

Economic management

If you want to know why Bill Clinton comes as high as fifteenth in the C-SPAN poll of presidential greatness, the answer is because of his economic management. In this part of the poll, Clinton finished third behind only Washington and Lincoln. What appears here as Table 6.4 first appeared in the 2001 edition of this publication in a chapter entitled 'The Clinton presidency assessed'. Clinton had fought the 1992 election with the slogan 'It's the economy, stupid!' He inherited a country so deep in economic difficulties that an independent candidate, Ross Perot, had run as a third-party candidate on that very issue and had won just shy of 20 million votes. But the figures in Table 6.4 speak for themselves, none more so than the fact that Clinton presided over the nation as a $290 billion federal budget deficit was turned into a $123 billion surplus.

Table 6.4 The economic state of the nation, 1993–2000

	1993	2000
Unemployment rate	7.3%	4.1%
Poverty rate	14.8%	12.7%
Inflation rate	2.9%	2.7%
Median income (in 1998 dollars)	$17,249	$20,120
Mortgage rate	8.0%	7.7%
Federal budget balance	–$290 billion	+$123 billion
Dow Jones Industrial Average	3,242	11,477
Minimum hourly wage	$4.25	$5.15

Moral authority

But if you want to know why, after all that, Bill Clinton came as low as fifteenth in the C-SPAN poll, the answer is because of his lack of moral authority. In this category, Clinton finished at number 38 – with just five presidents below him in the rankings. Writing at the time, Elizabeth Drew – for 19 years the Washington correspondent of the *New Yorker* magazine – wrote of Clinton:

> The presidency must have a certain aura of majesty and mystique. Clinton's lack of dignity, not to mention his sexual recklessness, was an assault on the office itself.

One wonders what Ms Drew would say of the forty-fifth president in this matter.

Relations with Congress

Because presidents can do so little without the consent of Congress, relations with Congress are a critical area for a would-be great president. They're the reason why Lyndon Johnson ends up in the top ten greats. He ranks number 1 in terms of relations with Congress. Equally, relations with Congress hurt Jimmy Carter (33) and Richard Nixon (37). For Johnson, 24 years on Capitol Hill before becoming vice president in 1961 were how he knew both how Congress worked and the people who worked it. He had served ten years in the Democratic leadership in the Senate. By contrast, Nixon had served only six years in Congress and Jimmy Carter had never served at all.

But all that having been said, we must secondly ask the question of whether we should still talk of 'presidential greatness' or whether it is a term that sits uncomfortably in a democratic federal system of government based on the principles of separation of powers, checks and balances, and limited government.

Should we still talk of presidential greatness?

The problem with talk of presidential greatness is that it sits awkwardly with a democratic form of government. The term seems merely to accentuate an unbridgeable divide between the leader and the people. Greatness is much more compatible with monarchy than with presidential government. Those of us familiar with our earlier European history will remember that Alexander, Peter, Frederick and even Catherine were all 'great'. But who would want to elect any of them as president of the United States?

If one thinks back to the presidency of FDR or those of the Cold War, the American president – alone – would attend summit meetings with his Soviet counterpart and make what were sometimes little more than unilateral decisions. The president spoke for 'America' with little regard for the views of the American public. Think of Kennedy eyeball-to-eyeball with Khrushchev over Cuba in 1962, or of Reagan bargaining with Gorbachev at the Reykjavik Summit in 1986. One might ask whether the term 'presidential greatness' is something of an oxymoron. Indeed, when Donald Trump held a meeting with Vladimir Putin of Russia in July 2018 attended only by interpreters, there was some degree of consternation even among some members of his own administration and party.

Second, on a related point, were those presidents deemed as 'great' democratically great? In some respects, all of the great four – Washington, Jefferson, Lincoln and FDR – come up short in this respect. After all, FDR for all his apparent greatness was the same man who on 19 February 1942 issued Executive Order 9066, thereby forcing 120,000 Americans of Japanese ancestry to live in internment camps until the end of the war.

Third, does talk of presidential greatness over-simplify a much more complicated issue? For there to be great leadership, there also needs to be great 'followership'. And there also need to be the circumstances that can foster so-called presidential greatness. In his 2014 book *The End of Greatness*, David Miller suggests that there needs to be a coincidence of three factors to facilitate an opportunity for great leadership. Miller calls these character, capacity and crisis. Character comprises unique public and private aspects that drive effective leadership. Capacity, according to Miller, is the know-how and ability to choose the right advisers, and to manage Congress, the party, the press. Both of these ingredients are partly determined by the president themselves. But Miller's third C, crisis, is of course mostly outside of the president's control. For Miller, this is a crisis that severely threatens the nation for a sustained period of time and sets the stage for historic change — something we discussed above.

Fourth, are great presidents only great in the memory? Maybe that's what Hamilton was warning us of when he talked about 'monuments of gratitude'. Is greatness more about legacy than contemporary achievement? After all, presidential greatness can ebb and flow. Some presidents — such as Truman, Eisenhower, Carter and George W. Bush — are more highly regarded now than they were just after they left office. Likewise, others find their reputations tarnish as their grand reforms fail to stand the test of time, or their much vaunted economic growth turns out to be somewhat ephemeral.

So we've looked at the factors that can lead to presidential greatness, and we've studied some of the paradoxes and limitations of this idea. Thirdly and finally, we address the question of why the days of presidential greatness might be over.

Why might the days of presidential greatness be over?
It's possible to suggest four reasons why the days of presidential greatness might be over. First, it's certainly true that since the days of FDR's presidency (1933– 45) Americans' expectations of their presidents have risen while the president's capacity to deliver has diminished. For a start, just think of all the policy areas that today's presidents must deliver on, that would have been quite unknown to the 'greats' of the nineteenth and early twentieth centuries. When FDR occupied the Oval Office there were just nine executive departments. By Johnson's time there were 11, by Carter's it was 13, and now it's 15. FDR spent little or no time on healthcare, education, energy, drugs, space or the environment.

And not only are expectations up, but capacity to deliver is down. For FDR's 12 years in the White House, his own Democrats controlled both houses of Congress for all 12 years. So-called 'divided government' was a rarity. Today, it's the norm — though not initially for President Trump. And FDR didn't just have a majority: for four years the Democrats had 69 seats in the Senate, and that figure rose to 76 in the 75th Congress (1937–38).

Second, the world and the country have changed. Crises are more long term, complicated and intractable. The one, visible enemy that was the Soviet Union imploded, only to be replaced by a multiplicity of faceless, stateless and borderless threats. Enemies are less obvious. The way Americans view the federal government

as a whole is much changed from the days of FDR, Kennedy and Johnson. Then, the federal government was seen as mostly effective, necessary and beneficial to the lives of ordinary Americans. Today, the federal government is seen by most no longer as an institution for the achievement of common goals, but as an alien body that stands between the citizenry and the realisation of their individual ambitions.

And another thing. During the nineteenth and early twentieth centuries, the national stage was smaller. The number of competing voices was fewer. Now, the president is just another voice in a cacophony of voices. It's not just ABC, NBC and CBS that the president has to play to now, but CNN, Fox, blogs, talk radio, the internet – and Twitter.

I'm reminded of comments that President Bill Clinton somewhat unwisely made in a live press conference in April 1995. The Republicans had just taken control of both houses of Congress, and only one of the three terrestrial TV channels had agreed to carry the President's news conference. So a questioner asked: 'Mr President, do you worry about making sure that your voice is heard in the coming months?' Here's his reply:

> No. Because, the Constitution gives me relevance. The power of our ideas gives me relevance. The record we have built up over the last two years gives it relevance. The President is relevant here.

The next day, the *Washington Post* carried a cartoon of a family asleep in front of a huge TV – even the cat was asleep – and on that huge TV is Bill Clinton saying, 'But I **AM** relevant!' And *Time* magazine summed up the President's predicament with its infamous cover story of 'The Incredible Shrinking President'.

Third, there has been the rise of what we call the partisan presidency. Partisanship has increased in the United States not only in the way people vote but also in the ideological stance of the two parties – especially of the Republicans – both in the country and in Congress, and this has affected the way Americans view their president. As a result, it seems doubtful now that any president could be regarded as 'great' by Americans of both parties. Presidents are now presidents of only half of America. Republicans would say that Ronald Reagan and George W. Bush were 'great presidents' (at least with a small 'g'), while Democrats would say the same about Clinton and Obama. But look at the way the other party views those presidents and the increase over the past three decades or so of what we call the partisan gap in presidential approving ratings.

And fourth, and finally, the Constitution was never meant to engender presidential – or any other – 'greatness'. We must also bear in mind that we might have regarded Washington, Jefferson, Lincoln and maybe both Roosevelts as 'great presidents' because they stood out in a sea of presidential mediocrity. After all, many presidents might look 'great' if put alongside Millard Fillmore, James Buchanan, Calvin Coolidge and Herbert Hoover, at a time when for most of history, the office of the presidency was on the periphery of national politics.

Conclusions

So, to conclude, in the spirit of the framers and in the context of the current age of hyper-partisanship, maybe we should look for presidents who are facilitators rather than great leaders, who think transactional rather than transformational, think good rather than great — or at least great with a small 'g'. But then maybe after a year in which the new incumbent of the office has boasted of his making everything 'great again', the presidency might be one of the many exceptions to that re-creation of greatness. And maybe, after all, the words 'great' and 'president' are unlikely to appear next to each other in a sentence for at least the next two years.

Questions

1 Why do different polls ranking presidents come up with very different results?
2 Why are the two columns in Table 6.2 so different?
3 How much of a link does the author suggest exists between presidential greatness and serving two consecutive full terms?
4 What is the link between crisis management and presidential greatness? Explain the quotation by Chris Matthews.
5 Why was Bill Clinton so highly rated for economic management?
6 What other factors are suggested that may affect presidential greatness?
7 What are the problems with talking about presidential greatness?
8 What reasons are suggested for why the days of presidential greatness may be over?
9 Given the factors discussed in this chapter, make an assessment of how far President Trump might be regarded as a great president.

Chapter 7

Looking ahead to 2020

What you need to know

- Presidential elections are held every four years in years divisible by 4: 2012, 2016, 2020, etc.
- The two major parties select their candidates through a series of state-based primaries and caucuses.
- A presidential primary is a state-based election to choose a party's candidate for the presidency.
- Presidential caucuses are a series of state-based meetings to choose a party's candidate for the presidency.
- Primaries and caucuses have two functions: to show support for potential candidates among ordinary voters; to choose delegates to vote for a particular candidate at the party's national convention.
- Super-delegates are appointed automatically as uncommitted delegates to the Democratic national convention by virtue of being elected politicians or senior party officials. (Republicans don't have super-delegates.)
- Super Tuesday is a Tuesday — usually at the beginning of March — when a number of states coincide their presidential primaries and caucuses to try to gain influence in the presidential nominating process.

It may look a little previous to write a chapter on the 2020 presidential election when it's still almost two years away. But in today's American politics we live in an era of the almost permanent campaign — and that's certainly the case with the current incumbent, who seems to see the top priority of his first term as campaigning for a second. After all, President Trump formally launched his candidacy for 2020 on 17 February 2017 — less than a month after taking office! To put that in perspective, President Obama formally launched his re-election campaign for 2012 on 4 April 2011 — two months into his third year in office.

The incumbent president and his party

For an incumbent president running for re-election, there's one simple rule of thumb — avoid any serious challengers in the primaries. Presidents Nixon (1972), Reagan (1984), Clinton (1996), Bush (2004) and Obama (2012) all did — and all went on to be re-elected to a second term. Presidents Ford (1976), Carter (1980) and Bush (1992) did not (see Figure 7.1) — and all were subsequently defeated in their re-election bid.

In 1976, President Ford faced a feisty challenge from former California governor Ronald Reagan. Although Ford won the primaries — just — he lost in November to

Jimmy Carter. Four years later, President Carter faced an equally powerful challenge from Senator Ted Kennedy. Carter won the primaries but lost in November to Ronald Reagan. Then in 1992, President George H.W. Bush faced a significant challenge in the Republican primaries from former White House aide and political commentator Pat Buchanan. Although Bush won every primary and caucus, Buchanan won more than 20% of the votes in 18 contests – topping 30% in New Hampshire, Colorado, Georgia, Florida and Rhode Island, and garnering nearly 3 million votes. It was enough to damage the President, who went on to lose to Bill Clinton in November.

Token opposition is not nearly so damaging. So, for example, in 1972, Congressman John Ashcroft of Ohio won just over 5% of the votes in the Republican primaries against President Nixon, but he never won more than 9% in any contest. Nixon sailed to a 49-state victory over Senator George McGovern in November.

So for Donald Trump, the absolute essential for 2020 must be to unite the Republican Party behind him and stop any high-profile Republicans from running in the primaries. We need, therefore, to ask two questions. First, is a primary challenge to Trump likely? You might think that the obvious answer to this question is 'yes' – because Trump is such a controversial figure and says, does and tweets controversial things. But that misses the point that, as of the time of writing, despite all of Trump's gaffes, controversies, scandals, outrages and untruths, his standing among Republicans is still sky high. In a poll for National Public Radio and the *PBS NewsHour* in late July 2018, 84% of self-identified Republicans said they approved of the job Donald Trump was doing as president. And among so-called 'strong Republicans' that figure rose to 91% with only 4% disapproving. And so long as President Trump continues to preside over a prospering economy, those figures don't look like changing a whole lot. So any challenger would have very few disgruntled Republicans to work with.

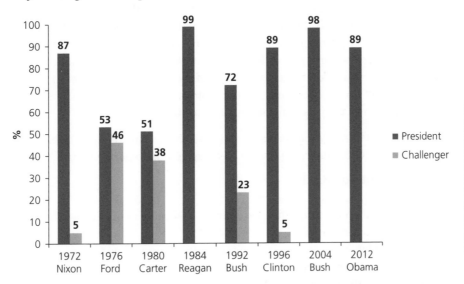

Figure 7.1 Share of primary votes by incumbent presidents seeking re-election, 1972–2012

Second, if — and it's a big if — there were to be a challenge, who are the possible candidates? Well, quite a few of Trump's primary opponents from 2016 have already said publicly that they won't be challenging the President in the Republican primaries — Marco Rubio, Chris Christie, Rand Paul, Scott Walker and Ted Cruz. Another two of Trump's Republican opponents from 2016 — Ben Carson and Rick Perry — are serving in Trump's cabinet, so rule them out. And the Republicans' 2012 presidential nominee Mitt Romney was elected to the Senate in the 2018 midterm elections. But there are two significant 'establishment' Republicans who, if they were to challenge Trump, could possibly pose a threat to the President — John Kasich and Jeb Bush.

Kasich — the former congressman and governor of Ohio — was the last to withdraw from the 2016 Republican primaries, by which time he had collected over 4 million votes and 161 delegates. Unlike most of the other 2016 candidates, Kasich never endorsed Trump and, despite the fact that the Republicans' national convention of 2016 was held in his home state, he never attended. Bush, the former Florida governor and younger brother of George W. Bush, would clearly have huge name recognition and an organisational base. But his 2016 campaign was lacklustre.

There are other names out there — notably Senator Ben Sasse of Nebraska, and former senators Jeff Flake of Arizona and Bob Corker of Tennessee — but whether they could ever mount a serious challenge to President Trump is highly debatable.

So what about the Democrats?

Another rule of thumb about presidential nominating contests is that the challenging party will almost always have a longer list of contestants than the party that controls the White House — especially in years like 2020 when the incumbent president is seeking re-election. So expect a much longer list of Democratic hopefuls than on the Republican side. The difficulty this far out from the start of the contest is discerning who the likely big-hitters will be. Writing in this publication 12 years ago — the same distance ahead of the 2008 presidential election — I listed whom I saw as the five most likely Democratic candidates for that election and Barack Obama was not one of them, though he did get a mention among the 'dark horse contenders' in the chapter's penultimate sentence! So what follows now comes with a significant health warning.

Undeterred, here are my four picks for the possible 'A team' of likely Democratic candidates for 2020. They are quite a mixed bag and in no particular order.

Vice President Joe Biden
Strengths
- congressional and White House experience — 36 years in the Senate and 8 years as vice president
- appeals to blue-collar voters, to whom Hillary Clinton failed to appeal in 2016 and many of whom voted for Donald Trump
- campaigning and oratorical skills
- personally likeable

Weaknesses

- age – if elected, he would be 78 at his inauguration
- can be a bit of a loose cannon, especially when he ad libs in public appearances

Senator Bernie Sanders

Strengths

- built up a loyal and devoted following in the 2016 primaries, winning over 13 million votes
- appeals to liberal and progressive wings of the party
- campaigning and oratorical skills

Weaknesses

- age – he's a year older than Biden
- no executive branch experience
- would have very limited appeal to independent voters in the general election
- comes from one of the smallest states – Vermont

Senator Elizabeth Warren

Strengths

- feisty campaigner: not afraid to stand up to and take on Donald Trump
- will have served eight years in the Senate
- would pick up the mantle of Hillary Clinton as the leading female candidate for the presidency

Weaknesses

- limited appeal to independents
- would find it difficult to compete against Sanders in the primaries, as they would be targeting the same kind of voters – indeed, she is unlikely to run if Sanders runs
- Republicans would easily paint her as a liberal

Senator Cory Booker

Strengths

- age – he would be 51 by Election Day
- experience – seven years as Mayor of Newark, New Jersey; six years in the Senate
- as a leading African-American politician, he's close to the Obamas

Weaknesses

- not as high profile nationwide as Biden, Sanders or Warren
- is America ready to elect its second African-American president just four years after President Obama left office?

And then there are the dark horses: senators Kirsten Gillibrand of New York, Kamala Harris of California and Amy Klobuchar of Minnesota; former governors Terry McAuliffe of Virginia, Martin O'Malley of Maryland and Deval Patrick of Massachusetts; the former mayor of San Antonio and one-time secretary of

housing and urban development Julian Castro; and Governor John Hickenlooper of Colorado. Somewhere among that Democratic dozen ought to be President Trump's challenger in 2020.

Democrats make changes to the nominating process

After the 2016 presidential nomination race, supporters of Bernie Sanders felt aggrieved that their candidate had been disadvantaged by the system. That said, the supporters of Hillary Clinton had some gripes too. Once the dust had settled, the Democrats set up a commission — the grandly named Unity Reform Commission (URC) — to 'study and address concerns that arose regarding the presidential nominating process'. The task the Commission was given was 'to ensure that the process is accessible, transparent and inclusive' — all Democratic buzzwords. The Commission held five public meetings during 2017 and heard testimony from a wide range of interested parties — professional politicians and party members as well as grassroots supporters. And the two issues they most significantly addressed were the role of super-delegates at the convention and the role of caucuses in the nominating system. Let's consider each in turn.

Super-delegates

Super-delegates first appeared at the Democratic national party convention in 1984 and are a Democrats-only phenomenon. Their purpose was to bring back so-called 'peer review' to the presidential nominating system. In the early 1970s, the party bosses — senior and powerful professional politicians who had virtually controlled the presidential nominating system in the 'smoke-filled rooms' — had been removed from the process and in their place had come ordinary delegates chosen by voters in the presidential primaries and caucuses. The trouble was that these folk knew little about the candidates themselves, nor did they know much about the qualities required in a president. As a result, the Democrats chose candidates who were not from the party establishment — George McGovern (1972) and Jimmy Carter (1976). So in 1984, the Democrats brought back the professional politicians — senators, congressmen, governors, big city mayors and the like — as super-delegates to be uncommitted delegates at the convention, casting their votes not on the basis of votes in the primaries, but on their own political experience and judgement. Their votes made up some 15% of the total delegate votes.

But for over 20 years, they played no significant role in the Democrats' presidential nominating process — until 2008. By this time, they made up around 19% of the total delegate votes, and they played a significant role in choosing Barack Obama over Hillary Clinton as the party's presidential candidate. Obama and Clinton ran neck-and-neck through the primaries, at the end of which Obama's lead in committed delegates chosen in the primaries was only around 60, out of over 3,500. This meant it was the votes of the uncommitted super-delegates who would decide the nomination, and they broke decisively for Obama, therefore delivering him the nomination. This caused some concerns within the party but little was done other than to reduce the proportion of super-delegate votes — back to around 15% of the total.

The controversy over super-delegates boiled over in 2016 when, yet again, they played a decisive role in choosing the candidate – this time preferring Hillary Clinton (the establishment candidate) over Bernie Sanders (the insurgent candidate). As Figure 7.2 shows, whereas Sanders had won 46% of the pledged delegates in the primaries and caucuses, thereby running Clinton quite close, he won a mere 7% of the super-delegates. Bernie Sanders' supporters were outraged and demanded change to what they saw as an outdated and undemocratic system.

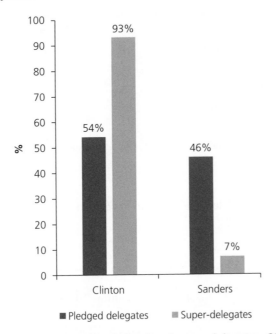

Figure 7.2 Democratic pledged and super-delegates, 2016

The unfairness and undemocratic nature of the system in 2016 can be even more easily seen by considering five states in which Sanders beat Clinton in the primary or caucuses (see Table 7.1). In these five states, Sanders won 159 of the 274 (58%) pledged delegates awarded proportionally on the result of the primary or caucuses, with Clinton winning the remaining 115 (or 42%). But of the 46 super-delegates from those five states, 43 (93%) would vote for Clinton and just 3 for Sanders. In three of these states – Rhode Island, Indiana and Carolina – Sanders picked up no super-delegate votes at all. And in Rhode Island, Clinton – despite having lost the primary by 11 percentage points – ended up winning more delegates from the state than Bernie Sanders. Furthermore, Table 7.2 shows the overwhelming level of support for Clinton amongst all the categories of super-delegates.

Table 7.1 Delegates won by Sanders and Clinton in selected states, 2016

State	Candidate	Popular vote (%)	Pledged delegates	Super-delegates
New Hampshire	Bernie Sanders	60.1	15	1
	Hillary Clinton	37.7	9	6
Minnesota	Bernie Sanders	61.6	46	2
	Hillary Clinton	38.4	31	12
Rhode Island	Bernie Sanders	54.7	13	0
	Hillary Clinton	43.1	11	9
Indiana	Bernie Sanders	52.5	44	0
	Hillary Clinton	47.5	39	7
Colorado	Bernie Sanders	59.0	41	0
	Hillary Clinton	40.3	25	9

At the Democratic national convention, the final delegate count was:
- Hillary Clinton 2,842
- Bernie Sanders 1,865

But without the super-delegates, it would have been:
- Hillary Clinton 2,272
- Bernie Sanders 1,821

Table 7.2 Super-delegate support by category, 2016

	Hillary Clinton	Bernie Sanders
Party leaders	17	1
Governors	20	0
Senators	45	2
House members	177	7
National Committee members	311	34
Totals	570	44

The URC recommendations, which are likely to be in place for the 2020 Democratic nominating contest, could make significant changes regarding both the number of super-delegates – which could be slashed in half – and their potential influence in voting. What the URC is recommending is that if no candidate has secured the necessary number of delegate votes from the state primaries and caucuses, super-delegates would not be able to vote in the first ballot at the convention. Under these circumstances, super-delegates could vote only from the second ballot in order to rectify an unresolved first ballot vote. We will need to keep an eye on these developments as we move closer to election year.

The role of caucuses

If the Sanders' delegates in 2016 were angry over the super-delegates, the Clinton supporters — both in 2008 and 2016 — were upset about the role of the caucuses. Their candidate did significantly worse in caucus states than in states that held a primary in both years. In 2016, Clinton lost 12 of the 14 states that held caucuses and of the two she won, Iowa saw her with a winning margin of less than 1 percentage point. She lost the caucuses in Idaho, Utah and Alaska by, respectively, 57, 60 and 64 percentage points. The trouble with caucuses is that they attract an even smaller and more unrepresentative group of voters than primaries. Caucuses — which are meetings held across the state — attract the more politically and ideologically committed. They also discourage participation among those who cannot, for reasons of work, infirmity, disability, age or family commitments, attend the meeting. Whereas in a primary, one merely has to call into the voting station for a few minutes at any time during a (usually) 10–11-hour opening time, caucuses are held in the evening and often last for two or three hours.

The URC report therefore stated:

> At a time when voting rights are under attack…many are concerned that caucuses disenfranchise voters, such as seniors, members of the military, working families, students, and parents of young children, who are not able to attend a caucus meeting or spend hours while internal meeting processes continue in order to exercise their right to participate in the presidential nominating process.

The Commission therefore instructed its state parties that use caucuses to 'find new and better ways to ensure broad participation'. As a result of the URC report, even by the time of writing, Democrats in four states — Maine, Minnesota, Idaho and Utah — were making plans to change from holding caucuses in 2016 to holding a primary in 2020.

The primary calendar takes shape

At the time of writing — some 16 months before the primaries and caucuses begin in 2020 — the nominating calendar is beginning to look a lot like that of 2016. The process will kick off with the Iowa caucuses on the first Monday in February — that will be 3 February 2020, the corresponding date to 2016. Then, again as in 2016, the New Hampshire primaries for both parties will follow eight days later, followed by contests in Nevada and South Carolina later that month.

Super Tuesday will in all probability once again be held on the first Tuesday in March, but it looks likely to be even more 'super' than in 2016 with California moving its primary to that date. In 2016, the California primary was not held until June, so that's a significant example of a return to front loading. North Carolina also looks likely to advance its primary date by two weeks compared with 2016 — to join the Super Tuesday states. As in 2016, there looks like being a Mid-Atlantic/Northeast regional primary on the last Tuesday in April, featuring Connecticut, Delaware, Maryland, Pennsylvania and Rhode Island.

National party conventions

As for the national party conventions, the Democrats have yet to decide on a venue. At the time of writing, there is a short-list of three — Houston, Miami and Milwaukee. But they have fixed the date — 13–16 July 2020.

Tradition holds that the party currently holding the White House holds their convention after that of the challenging party. The Republicans will hold their 2020 convention in Charlotte, North Carolina, between 24 and 27 August.

Questions

1 What does Figure 7.1 show about the one rule of thumb for an incumbent president running for re-election?
2 Which possible challengers might President Trump face in the Republican primaries in 2020?
3 Briefly summarise the Democratic Party's front-runners for 2020.
4 What is the Unity Reform Commission and why was it set up?
5 What do Figure 7.2 and Table 7.1 show about problems regarding super-delegates back in 2016?
6 What possible reforms may be made in 2020 regarding super-delegates?
7 Why are some state Democratic parties switching from caucuses to a primary in 2020?

Chapter 8

What's wrong with the US Constitution?

In a recent article in *Politics Review* ('Does the US Constitution Still Work?', Vol. 28, No. 1, September 2018, pp. 18–21), I looked at four particular areas where one could make out a strong case that the US Constitution does not work well – gun control, the Electoral College, war-making powers and impeachment. But there are other areas one could consider. So in asking the question here – 'What's wrong with the US Constitution?' – we will consider other areas in which one could suggest that there are indeed things wrong with the US Constitution. Specifically, we shall consider seven other areas in which the Constitution throws up some significant problems. Most of them concern the three institutions of American government – the Congress, the presidency and the Supreme Court. And at the outset, let me gratefully acknowledge that the idea for this chapter came to me having just read Robert Singh's excellent new book, *In Defense of the United States Constitution* (New York: Routledge, 2019). Professor Singh analyses these and many other issues in his scholarly yet highly accessible book, in which he puts forward a cogent argument in defence of the Constitution – notwithstanding its clear deficiencies.

Constitutional amendment

The amendment process itself is a good place to start. After all, if the Constitution – mostly written towards the close of the eighteenth century – needs updating, the most obvious way to do that is by formal amendment. But as Figure 8.1 shows, that process was made deliberately complex. As a result, most proposed constitutional amendments fall at the first hurdle – in either the House of Representatives or the Senate.

On 12 April 2018, the House voted on a bill 'proposing a balanced budget amendment to the Constitution of the United States'. The Yeas were 233; the Nays were 184. That's a majority of 49 in favour of passage. But, of course, because of the Constitution's requirement that votes to propose constitutional amendments must pass by a majority of at least two-thirds – in both houses – this proposal, like nearly all the ones before it on the same matter, failed. With 417 members voting, there would have had to be 278 voting 'yes'. The bill fell 45 votes short. The trouble is, that's par for the course. Since 1999, in fact, 134 separate balanced budget amendments have been formally introduced in either the House or the Senate, making it the single most popular subject for amendment proposals during the past two decades (see Figure 8.2). Congress came closest to sending such an amendment to the states for ratification in January 1995 when the House passed one by 300 votes to 132 – comfortably above the required two-thirds

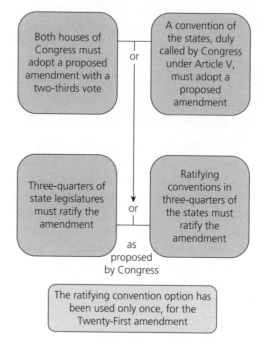

Figure 8.1 Constitutional amendment procedure

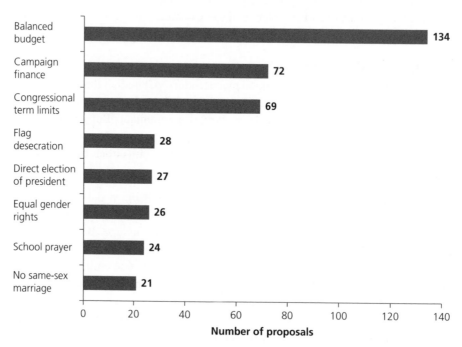

Figure 8.2 Subjects of constitutional amendment proposals in Congress, 1999–2018

Source: Pew Research Center, 12 April 2018

majority. But it failed twice in the Senate – in March 1995 by 65–35 and in June 1996 by 64–35 – on both occasions falling just two votes short of the required super-majority.

Although Congress can also call a convention of the states to propose amendments, this can occur only if two-thirds of the states request such a convention and that threshold has never been reached. Of the roughly 12,000 amendments proposed since the Constitutional Convention of 1787 that wrote the original Constitution, only 33 have gone to the states for ratification and, of those, 27 have made it into the Constitution itself. That represents around 0.2% of all proposals! So despite widespread public disquiet about a number of the provisions of the US Constitution, the realistic chance of amending any of them is virtually nil – the more so in today's partisan political atmosphere.

Presidential succession

Article II, Section 1, Paragraph 6 of the Constitution states:

> In Case of the Removal of the President from Office, or of his Death, Resignation, or Inability to discharge the Powers and Duties of the said Office, the same shall devolve on the Vice President, and *Congress may by Law* provide for the Case of Removal, Death, Resignation or Inability, both of the President and Vice President, declaring what Officer shall then act as President. (emphasis added)

So the framers of the Constitution provided that the vice president should be first in order of presidential succession, but they left it up to Congress to establish the rest of the order of succession. Three times, Congress has passed legislation dealing with presidential succession.

- In 1792, Congress passed a law placing the president pro tempore of the Senate – by custom the longest-serving member of the majority party in the Senate – as first in line behind the vice president.
- In 1886, Congress passed another law negating the 1792 Act and placing the heads of the cabinet departments in order of their creation in immediate line of presidential succession, thereby placing the secretary of state first in line behind the vice president.
- In 1947, Congress passed a third law placing the Speaker of the House first behind the vice president, followed by the Senate's president pro tempore, followed by the cabinet officers, again by departmental seniority.

It is therefore the third of these laws that is applicable today. But these provisions do present a problem because they place 78-year-old Nancy Pelosi (House Speaker) and 85-year-old Charles Grassley (Senate President Pro Tempore) as respectively second and third in line to the presidency. One cannot really believe that either of those two people would be thought likely to win the presidential office by election. Neither of them has ever been a presidential or vice-presidential candidate for their party. And constitutional problems regarding presidential succession extend even further.

Presidential disability

The Twenty-Fifth Amendment was added to the Constitution in 1967. Among other things it provided for the president either to be able to declare himself disabled or to be declared disabled by others. Presidents have declared themselves temporarily disabled on three occasions:

- 1985 (13 July) — President Ronald Reagan during a brief hospitalisation
- 2002 (29 June) — President George W. Bush undergoing a colonoscopy
- 2007 (21 July) — President George W. Bush undergoing a colonoscopy

On all three occasions, the vice president became acting president for just a few hours. With that provision there is no problem. The problem arises with Paragraph 4 of the Amendment (see Box 8.1), a section of the Constitution much talked about since Donald Trump was elected in 2016. David Frum, a conservative author and former speechwriter for President George W. Bush, wrote just eight days after Mr Trump's election: 'We're going to be talking a lot more about the Twenty-Fifth Amendment in the months ahead.'

Box 8.1　**The Twenty-Fifth Amendment, Paragraph 4**

Whenever the Vice President and a majority of either the principal officers of the executive departments or of such other body as Congress may by law provide, transmit to the President pro tempore of the Senate and the Speaker of the House of Representatives their written declaration that the President is unable to discharge the powers and duties of the office, the Vice President shall immediately assume the powers and duties of the office as Acting President.

Then came the disclosure in an anonymous editorial in the *New York Times* in the late summer of 2018 that 'given the instability [of the President] many witnessed, there were early whispers within the cabinet of invoking the 25th Amendment' but 'no one wanted to precipitate a constitutional crisis'. Then came the revelation that the deputy attorney general, Rod Rosenstein, had discussed the possibility of invoking the amendment's fourth paragraph.

But the amendment raises significant problems. For example, there is no clarity concerning what 'unable to discharge the powers and duties of the office' means. It was devised — following the Kennedy assassination — for a situation when the president might be in a coma or dangerously ill. Could it be applied to a president whose behaviour seemed merely erratic and who would fight such an attempt to invoke the provision?

Presidential qualifications

Article II, Section 1, Paragraph 5 of the Constitution lays down three qualifications for those who would become president: to be a natural-born American citizen; at least 35 years old; and resident within the United States for at least 14 years. It seems highly unlikely that a constitution written today would include such a curious collection of requirements. According to Professor Singh, 'there is a compelling logic to relaxing these [requirements]'. He continues:

> Given the incredible demands of a unique office, it makes sense to maximise, not limit, the candidate pool...Requiring a candidate to have resided in the United States for fourteen years seems excessive, especially in an era when many Americans live and work abroad for some periods of their lives. And the danger of a 'non-naturalized' citizen serving as a foreign agent or exchanging influence for gifts or personal enrichment now looks more than a little ironic.

As for the minimum age requirement, there seems no logical reason to choose 35 years. After all, just four years before the founding fathers gathered at Philadelphia and wrote these requirements, William Pitt had become British prime minister at the age of 24. Indeed, some might argue that in the era of Ronald Reagan and Donald Trump, a *maximum* age limit might be more relevant.

Presidential term limits

The Twenty-Second Amendment (1951) limited the president to serving two full terms. This was a direct result of Franklin D. Roosevelt having broken the convention — established by George Washington in 1796 — that presidents would seek re-election only once. FDR was first elected in 1932, but was re-elected three times — in 1936, 1940 and 1944. He died within three months of the start of his fourth term. The late Professor Anthony King wrote in 2012 that the two-term limit was an oddly 'anti-democratic' feature of the American political system — because it limits the choice of voters. For example, voters in 2001 and 2017 respectively were barred from choosing Bill Clinton or Barack Obama as their president despite the fact that both fulfilled the constitutional requirements laid down in Article II.

Robert Singh sees other problems with this. He believes that it leads to a lack of legislative productivity in a president's second term, as a president's 'lame-duck' status kicks in early into that final term. 'Despite prestige and power,' writes Singh, 'other actors increasingly see the president as exhausted and eye future horizons — the next midterms and the president's successor.' Forcing young, energetic and focused presidents into an early retirement seems to make little sense. Bill Clinton and Barack Obama were 54 and 55 respectively when they were forced to leave office after completing their allotted two terms.

Judicial life terms

While presidents are limited to just eight years in office, justices of the Supreme Court (and of all federal courts) are — courtesy of Article III — appointed for life 'during good behaviour'. In other words, short of impeachment, a justice of the Supreme Court can serve either until he or she voluntarily retires, or until they die. At the time of writing, Ruth Bader Ginsburg is still serving into the year in which she will celebrate her 86th birthday. And Justice Stephen Breyer will be 81 this year. On the other hand, Chief Justice William Rehnquist, who died in post in 2005 aged 80, was laid low with thyroid cancer for much of what proved to be his final year.

There are three problems here. First, can men and women of the age of Ginsburg, Breyer and Rehnquist be reasonably expected to cope with the demanding workload of a justice of the nation's highest court? Second, is there a danger that octogenarian justices become a kind of echo chamber for an age that has long passed? And third, the life tenure of justices clearly limits the turnover of the Court and thereby elevates the importance of any single nomination because they occur so rarely.

True, life tenure supposedly guarantees judicial independence. But, as Singh points out, 'the flip side is that [life] tenure also ensures unaccountability'. As a result, some scholars have suggested reforms such as a non-renewable 18-year term. This would result in a new appointment to the Supreme Court every two years. Every president would get to appoint two justices in a single term, and four in a two-term presidency. If one wanted to be truly radical, one might reform the nomination and confirmation process entirely, getting rid of the principle that the justices should be appointed by a politician and confirmed by politicians. Many states, after all, have their state judges nominated by independent commissions and subject to a mandatory retirement age – just like the judges of the UK Supreme Court.

Composition of the Senate

Article I, Section 3, Paragraph 1 of the Constitution states that 'the Senate of the United States shall be composed of two Senators from each State'. According to Professor Singh, 'nowhere is the Constitution more out of sync with democratic sensibilities than in allocating two senators per state regardless of population size'. What this means is that in 2017 California's estimated 39.5 million people were represented by two senators. At the same time, Wyoming's 579,315 people were represented by two senators – that's one senator for every 289,657 people. If California were to be awarded senators on the same basis, they would have not two senators but 136!

Here are three more consequences of the way the Constitution allocates seats in the Senate:

- The 21 smallest states, representing just 12% of the nation's population, have 42 senators between them.
- The 1.5 million people of North and South Dakota have twice the representation in the Senate compared with the 28 million people who live in Texas.
- If all 50 senators from the nation's 25 smallest states voted for a bill, and the vice president cast the tie-breaking vote, senators representing only 16% of Americans would have triumphed over those representing the remaining 84%.

Conclusion

In all these varied ways, it is possible to suggest that there are some significant things wrong with the US Constitution. But for every paragraph we write about what's wrong with the US Constitution, one could write at least a page on what is right with it – why it has and deserves to endure. It's also easy to blame the current all-too-apparent ills besetting the American polity on a (mainly) eighteenth-century document. But the Constitution has been the nation's guiding star through its inception, its westward expansion, a civil war, industrialisation, wars abroad and crises at home. It's survived Pearl Harbor and Vietnam. It's survived the Wall Street Crash and Watergate. It's survived Richard Nixon and it will survive Donald Trump. And as former President Bill Clinton liked to remark: 'The Constitution boils down to one thing: Let's have an argument, and then let's make a deal.' That's as true in 2019 as it was in 1789.

Questions

1 Why do most constitutional amendments fail?
2 What constitutional problems exist regarding presidential succession?
3 What problems does the Twenty-Fifth Amendment leave unanswered regarding presidential disability?
4 What changes could be made regarding presidential qualifications laid down in the Constitution?
5 Why have some called the two-term limit on the presidency 'anti-democratic'?
6 What are the drawbacks of life tenure in the federal judiciary?
7 What quirks does equal representation in the Senate for all 50 states throw up?
8 Despite these constitutional difficulties, what conclusion does the author come to regarding the US Constitution? Do you agree?
9 Try to explain the closing quotation from President Bill Clinton in your own words.

Chapter 9

The Brett Kavanaugh nomination

What you need to know

- The Supreme Court is made up of nine justices.
- They are appointed by the president and must be confirmed by the Senate by a simple majority vote.
- They serve for life, unless they are impeached and convicted or choose to retire.
- After the president announces his nominee, public hearings are held by the Senate Judiciary Committee.
- After those hearings conclude, the full Senate debates and votes on the nomination.

Justice Kennedy retires

Anthony Kennedy was appointed as a justice of the Supreme Court by President Ronald Reagan and took his seat on the bench in February 1988. He served for 30 years. Although appointed by Reagan as a 'conservative', Kennedy became increasingly seen as a 'centrist' – the justice who straddled the Court between four liberals and four conservatives. So this retirement gave President Trump the chance, by choosing a solid conservative to replace Kennedy, to swing the court to the right. Such opportunities to reshape the ideology of the Supreme Court come rarely (see Anthony J. Bennett, 'To what extent can a president reshape the Supreme Court?', *US Government & Politics Annual Update 2018*, Chapter 2). This is why the battle to confirm Kennedy's replacement was always going to be hotly contested on both sides of the political aisle. And the contest was made even hotter by the fact that this whole process was to be played out against the backdrop of the 2018 midterm elections, in which political control of both houses of Congress was at stake.

Choosing a successor

During the 2016 election, Donald Trump published a list of names of people who would be his shortlist of candidates for the Supreme Court if he won the election and if and when a Supreme Court vacancy occurred. After President Trump had nominated Neil Gorsuch to the Court in 2017, he added five more names to his list of potential candidates. It was from this list of '25 highly qualified potential nominees' that Judge Brett Kavanaugh was chosen.

At the time, the 53-year-old Kavanaugh was serving on the US Court of Appeals – the tier of courts just below the Supreme Court in the federal court structure.

He had been appointed to that court by President George W. Bush back in 2006, having previously served as White House staff secretary to President Bush. Kavanaugh's opinions on the appeals court clearly marked him out as a conservative judge who interpreted the Constitution in a strict and literal fashion, one who believed that the role of judges is to interpret the law, not 'make law' from the bench. In his younger days, Kavanaugh had been a clerk to Justice Kennedy at the Supreme Court (1993–94), where one of his fellow clerks was Neil Gorsuch – now to be one of his colleagues on the Supreme Court. After that, Kavanaugh worked for the independent counsel Kenneth Starr during Starr's investigation of President Bill Clinton that led to Clinton's impeachment.

On 2 July 2018, Kavanaugh was one of four federal judges to be interviewed personally interview by President Trump, and just one week later, the President announced his intention to nominate Judge Kavanaugh to replace Anthony Kennedy as a justice of the Supreme Court. The American Bar Association gave Kavanaugh a 'well qualified' rating.

At the White House ceremony to announce his nomination, Judge Kavanaugh wasted no time in declaring in the broadest of terms his judicial philosophy. 'My judicial philosophy is straightforward,' explained Judge Kavanaugh. 'A judge must be independent and must interpret the law, not make the law. A judge must interpret statutes as written, informed by history and tradition and precedent.' All this will have been music to the ears of Republican politicians and supporters, who saw Kavanaugh's choice of words as his reassurance that he intends to follow in the footsteps of justices such as Clarence Thomas and Samuel Alito. 'I believe that an independent judiciary is the crown jewel of our constitutional republic,' Kavanaugh continued. 'If confirmed by the Senate, I will keep an open mind in every case and I will always strive to preserve the Constitution of the United States and the American rule of law.'

Senate confirmation

When Anthony Kennedy had been nominated to the Supreme Court back in the 1980s, he had been confirmed by a vote in the Senate of 97–0. Such unanimity is a thing of the past and Kavanaugh's nomination would be the most keenly fought Supreme Court nomination in the Senate for well over a century. Having said that, all was going to plan until just before the Senate was due to vote.

The Senate Judiciary Committee scheduled four days of hearings on the nominee beginning on 4 September. The committee was made up of 21 members – 11 Republicans and 10 Democrats – and was chaired by Senator Chuck Grassley, a Republican from Iowa. But, as tends to be the case these days, the hearings elicited little of interest. Republican senators tended to throw softball questions at the nominee, while taking most of their allotted half-hours to make speeches in admiration of Kavanaugh. Democrats, on the other hand, tried to find fault with Kavanaugh's judicial record, questioning him on how he might rule on specific issues such as abortion and presidential power while the nominee answered with

vague generalities. Overall, the committee hearings failed to unearth anything of particular interest and it appeared that Kavanaugh would be duly confirmed.

Sexual assault allegations

The Senate Judiciary Committee was scheduled to vote on Kavanaugh's nomination on 20 September. But just four days before this, the media reported that Christine Blasey Ford, a psychology professor at Palo Alto University, California, had made an allegation against Kavanaugh that he had sexually assaulted her while the two were at a party during their time in high school back in the 1980s. This breathed new life into the campaign of those who had been opposing Judge Kavanaugh's appointment. Once the President said that he was standing by his nominee, despite the allegations, the Senate Judiciary Committee felt obliged to reopen its hearing, thereby postponing a full Senate vote.

> **Box 9.1 Professor Christine Blasey Ford timeline**
>
> - Early July: Ford contacts the *Washington Post* about her allegations, as well as contacting her member of Congress — Anna Eshoo (D-Cal.)
> - 20 July: Representative Anna Eshoo meets with Professor Ford and, convinced of her truthfulness, contacts the senior Democrat on the Senate Judiciary Committee, Dianne Feinstein of California.
> - August: Professor Ford takes a polygraph (lie-detector) test administered by a former FBI agent, who concludes that Ford is telling the truth. Professor Ford continues to insist on her anonymity, fearing a media firestorm if her name were to become public knowledge.
> - 16 September: after media reports of an anonymous accuser, Ford decides to go public with her allegations.
> - 21 September: President Trump publishes a tweet saying that if Ford's allegations about Kavanaugh were true, either she or her parents would have reported the matter at the time. Republican Senator Susan Collins of Maine, who was considered an undecided vote on the nomination, said she was appalled by the President's comment.
> - 27 September: the Senate Judiciary Committee reconvenes its hearings in order to hear testimony from both Professor Ford and Judge Kavanaugh regarding the allegations.

High Noon at the Senate Judiciary Committee

Following the escalation of events (see Box 9.1), the Senate Judiciary Committee convened a further day of hearings in order to hear testimony from both Professor Ford and Judge Kavanaugh. It was a day of high drama on Capitol Hill. Appearing at the hearing first, Professor Ford gave a detailed and graphic account of the alleged event some 35 years ago. She recalled details about the layout of the house, those present in the room while the alleged assault took place and, when asked, said she was '100% certain' that it was Brett Kavanaugh who had tried to rape her. She said that at one point during the attack, Kavanaugh had put his hand over her mouth to stop her screaming and that she thought he might, by accident, actually kill her.

Following her testimony, Ford was then questioned by each Democratic member of the committee. But the Republican senators — all men — opted to have their time for questions given over to questioning of Ford by a career prosecutor, Rachel Mitchell. The Republicans were anxious about the possible negative impact of the visuals of 11 men questioning Professor Ford over such allegations.

The most startling event of the day, however, was the testimony offered by Judge Kavanaugh, who appeared angry, emotional and at times deeply partisan in his remarks. After the traumatic events of the previous days, the emotion was understandable. But many baulked at the angry and partisan nature of some of Judge Kavanaugh's comments (see Box 9.2). Indeed, some thought that he had overstepped the mark by referring to the 'behaviour of several Democratic members of [the] committee' as 'an embarrassment'. His description of the confirmation process as 'a national disgrace' and 'a circus' might well have resonated with many impartial observers. But to suggest that Professor Ford's allegations against him were motivated by 'revenge on behalf of the Clintons' appeared to many to be partisan, absurd and without a shred of evidence. Many worried how someone who had made such partisan charges in public could preside on the nation's highest court.

| Box 9.2 | **Extracts from Judge Kavanaugh's testimony at the Senate Judiciary Committee, 27 September 2018** |

This confirmation process has become a national disgrace. The Constitution gives the Senate an important role in the confirmation process, but you have replaced advice and consent with search and destroy. The behaviour of several of the Democratic members of this committee at my hearing a few weeks ago was an embarrassment. But...when I did at least OK enough at the hearings that it looked like I might actually get confirmed, a new tactic was needed.

Some of you were lying in wait and had it ready. This first allegation was held in secret for weeks by a Democratic member of this committee, and by staff. It would be needed only if you couldn't take me out on the merits. When it was needed, this allegation was unleashed and publicly deployed over Dr Ford's wishes. And then — and then as no doubt was expected — if not planned — came a long series of false last-minute smears designed to scare me and drive me out of the process before any hearing occurred.

This whole two-week effort has been a calculated and orchestrated political hit, fuelled with apparent pent-up anger about President Trump and the 2016 election: fear that has been unfairly stoked about my judicial record; revenge on behalf of the Clintons; and millions of dollars from outside left-wing opposition groups. This is a circus. And as we all know, in the United States political system of the early 2000s, what goes around comes around.

I will not be intimidated into withdrawing from this process. You've tried hard. You've given it your all. No one can question your effort, but your coordinated and well-funded effort to destroy my good name and to destroy my family will not drive me out. The vile threats of violence against my family will not drive me out. You may defeat me in the final vote, but you'll never get me to quit. Never.

Consequences

The obvious consequence of all this was that Brett Kavanaugh was still confirmed as a justice of the Supreme Court. After a few days' further delay to facilitate a further FBI investigation of the charges against Kavanaugh, the Senate duly voted on the nomination. On 6 October, the Senate voted by 50 votes to 48 to confirm Kavanaugh. Of the 51 Republicans, 49 voted 'yes', Senator Steve Daines of Montana was absent attending his daughter's wedding, and Senator Lisa Murkowski of Alaska voted 'present'. Of the 49 Democrats, all voted 'no' except Senator Joe Manchin of West Virginia who voted 'yes' — the only senator to cross party lines on the vote. This made Kavanaugh's confirmation vote — by a margin of just two votes — the closest confirmation vote for a Supreme Court nominee since the confirmation of Stanley Matthews in 1881 by a vote of 24 to 23.

As for the consequences for the Supreme Court itself, they must wait for another day. But it seems likely that if Justice Kavanaugh proves to be a reliable conservative vote on the Court — joining Clarence Thomas, Samuel Alito and Neil Gorsuch — then Chief Justice John Roberts could become the new 'swing justice'. Might, therefore, the Republicans discover that elevating Brett Kavanaugh to the Supreme Court to replace Anthony Kennedy will have changed the ideological balance of the Court less than they had hoped? Only time will tell.

Questions

1 How did this vacancy on the Supreme Court occur?
2 Give two reasons why the confirmation of Judge Kavanaugh was going to be hotly contested.
3 Why did the initial hearings by the Senate Judiciary Committee elicit little of any interest?
4 What allegations then surfaced concerning Brett Kavanaugh? Who made these allegations?
5 Why did all 11 Republican senators decline to question Professor Ford directly following her testimony to the committee?
6 What was especially noteworthy — and to some troubling — about Judge Kavanaugh's testimony to the committee?
7 How close was the vote to confirm Brett Kavanaugh in the full Senate? To what extent was this a party-line vote?